LONGMAN
Preparation Course
for the
TOEFL® Test

iBT

SPEAKING

DEBORAH PHILLIPS

PEARSON
Longman

Longman Preparation Course for the TOEFL® Test: iBT Speaking

Pearson Education, 10 Bank Street, White Plains, NY 10606

Staff credits: The people who made up the *Longman Preparation Course for the TOEFL Test: iBT Speaking* team, representing editorial, production, design, and manufacturing, are: Rhea Banker, Angela M. Castro, Dave Dickey, Warren Fischbach, Pam Fishman, Nancy Flaggman, Patrice Fraccio, Lester Holmes, Katherine Keyes, Melissa Leyva, Lise Minovitz, Linda Moser, Michael Mone, Mary Rich, and Ken Volcjak.

Project editor: Helen B. Ambrosio
CD-ROM technical manager: Evelyn Fella
Text design adaptation: Page Designs International
Text composition: Page Designs International
Text photography: Hutchings Photography, Pearson Learning Group

Library of Congress Cataloging-in-Publication Data

Phillips, Deborah.
   Longman preparation course for the TOEFL(r) test : iBT speaking / Deborah Phillips. — 2nd ed.
       p. cm.
   Previous ed. published as: Longman preparation course for the TOEFL(r) test, 1st ed. 2006.
   Longman preparation course for the TOEFL(r): iBT will be published in four separate volumes: writing , reading, speaking, and listening.
   Includes bibliographical references.
   ISBN 978-0-13-612660-7 (student book with cd-rom) 1. English language—Textbooks for foreign speakers. 2. Test of English as a Foreign Language—Study guides. 3. English language—Examinations—Study guides. 4. English language—Spoken English. I. Title.
   PE1128.P4457 2007
   428.0076—dc22

                                        2007028891

PEARSON LONGMAN ON THE **WEB**

Pearsonlongman.com offers online resources for teachers and students. Access our Companion Websites, our online catalog, and our local offices around the world.

Visit us at **pearsonlongman.com**.

Printed in the United States of America
5 6 7 8 9 10—V001—16 15 14

CONTENTS

SPEAKING INTRODUCTION

ABOUT THIS COURSE

PURPOSE OF THE COURSE

This course is intended to prepare students for the Speaking section of the TOEFL® iBT (Internet-Based Test). It is based on the most up-to-date information available on the TOEFL iBT.

    Longman Preparation Course for the TOEFL Test: iBT Speaking can be used in a variety of ways, depending on the needs of the reader:

• It can be used as the *primary classroom text* in a course emphasizing preparation for the TOEFL iBT.

• It can be used as a *supplementary text* in a more general ESL/EFL course.

• Along with its companion audio program, it can be used as a tool for *individualized study* by students preparing for the TOEFL iBT outside of the ESL/EFL classroom.

WHAT IS IN THE BOOK

The book contains a variety of materials that together provide a comprehensive preparation course for the Speaking section of the TOEFL iBT:

• A **Speaking Diagnostic Pre-Test** for the Speaking section of the TOEFL iBT measures students' level of performance and allows students to determine specific areas of weakness.

• **Language Skills** for the Speaking section of the test provide students with a thorough understanding of the language skills that are regularly tested in the Speaking section of the TOEFL iBT.

• **Test-Taking Strategies** for the Speaking section of the test provide students with clearly defined steps to maximize their performance in this section of the test.

• **Exercises** provide practice of one or more speaking skills in a non-TOEFL format.

• **TOEFL Exercises** provide practice of one or more speaking skills in a TOEFL format.

• **TOEFL Review Exercises** provide practice of all of the speaking skills taught up to that point in a TOEFL format.

• A **Speaking Post-Test** for the Speaking section of the test measures the progress that students have made after working through the skills and strategies in the text.

• Eight **Speaking Mini-Tests** allow students to simulate the experience of taking actual Speaking test sections using shorter versions (approximately 10 minutes each) of the Speaking section of the test.

• Two **Speaking Complete Tests** allow students to simulate the experience of taking actual tests using full-length versions (approximately 20 minutes each) of the Speaking section of the test.

• **Scoring Information** allows students to determine their approximate TOEFL scores on the Speaking Diagnostic Pre-Test, Speaking Post-Test, Speaking Mini-Tests, and Speaking Complete Tests.

• **Skill-Assessment Checklists** allow students to monitor their progress in specific language skills on the Speaking Pre-Test, Speaking Post-Test, Speaking Mini-Tests, and Speaking Complete Tests so that they can determine which skills have been mastered and which skills require further study.

WHAT IS ON THE CD-ROM

The CD-ROM, with test items that are completely different from the questions in this book, includes a variety of materials that contribute to an effective preparation program for the Speaking section of the TOEFL iBT.

- An **Overview** describes the features of the CD-ROM.
- **Skills Practice** for the Speaking section provides students with the opportunity to review and master each of the speaking language skills on the test.
- Eight **Speaking Mini-Tests** allow students to simulate the experience of taking actual Speaking test sections using shorter versions (approximately 10 minutes each) of the Speaking section of the test.
- Two **Speaking Complete Tests** allow students to simulate the experience of taking actual Speaking test sections using full-length versions (approximately 20 minutes each) of the Speaking section of the test.
- **Answers** and **Explanations** for all Speaking skills practice and test items allow students to understand their errors and learn from their mistakes.
- **Skills Reports** relate the Speaking test items on the CD-ROM to the Speaking language skills presented in the book.
- **Results Reports** enable students to record and print out charts that monitor their progress on all skills practice and test items.
- A **Send Data** feature allows students to send their speaking results to the teacher.

The following chart describes the contents of the CD-ROM:

SKILLS PRACTICE		TESTS	
Speaking Skills 1–2	3 questions	Speaking Mini-Test 1	3 questions
Speaking Skills 3–4	3 questions	Speaking Mini-Test 2	3 questions
Speaking Skills 5–8	3 questions	Speaking Mini-Test 3	3 questions
Speaking Skills 9–12	3 questions	Speaking Mini-Test 4	3 questions
Speaking Skills 13–15	3 questions	Speaking Mini-Test 5	3 questions
Speaking Skills 16–18	3 questions	Speaking Mini-Test 6	3 questions
		Speaking Mini-Test 7	3 questions
		Speaking Mini-Test 8	3 questions
		Speaking Complete Test 1	6 questions
		Speaking Complete Test 2	6 questions

AUDIO RECORDINGS TO ACCOMPANY THE BOOK

The recording program that accompanies this book includes all of the recorded materials from the Speaking Diagnostic Pre-Test, Speaking Skills, Speaking Post-Test, Speaking Mini-Tests, and Speaking Complete Tests.

OTHER AVAILABLE MATERIALS

Longman publishes a full suite of materials for TOEFL preparation: materials for the paper TOEFL test and the iBT (Internet-Based Test), at both intermediate and advanced levels. Please contact Longman's website at www.longman.com for a complete list of available TOEFL products.

ABOUT THE TOEFL iBT

OVERVIEW OF THE TOEFL iBT

The TOEFL iBT is a test to measure the English proficiency and academic skills of nonnative speakers of English. It is required primarily by English-language colleges and universities. Additionally, institutions such as government agencies, businesses, or scholarship programs may require this test.

DESCRIPTION OF THE TOEFL iBT

The TOEFL iBT currently has the following four sections:

- The **Reading** section consists of three long passages and questions about the passages. The passages are on academic topics; they are the kind of material that might be found in an undergraduate university textbook. Students answer questions about stated details, inferences, sentence restatements, sentence insertion, vocabulary, pronoun reference function, and overall ideas.

- The **Listening** section consists of six long passages and questions about the passages. The passages consist of two student conversations and four academic lectures or discussions. The questions ask the students to determine main ideas, details, function, stance, inferences, and overall organization.

- The **Speaking** section consists of six tasks, two independent tasks and four integrated tasks. In the two independent tasks, students must answer opinion questions about some aspect of academic life. In the two integrated reading, listening, and speaking tasks, students must read a passage, listen to a passage, and speak about how the ideas in the two passages are related. In the two integrated listening and speaking tasks, students must listen to long passages and then summarize and offer opinions on the information in the passages.

- The **Writing** section consists of two tasks, one integrated task and one independent task. In the integrated task, students must read an academic passage, listen to an academic passage, and write about how the ideas in the two passages are related. In the independent task, students must write a personal essay.

The probable format of a TOEFL iBT is outlined in the following chart:

	iBT	**APPROXIMATE TIME**
READING	3 passages and 39 questions	60 minutes
LISTENING	6 passages and 34 questions	60 minutes
SPEAKING	6 tasks and 6 questions	20 minutes
WRITING	2 tasks and 2 questions	60 minutes

It should be noted that at least one of the sections of the test will include extra, uncounted material. Educational Testing Service (ETS) includes extra material to try out material for future tests. If you are given a longer section, you must work hard on all of the materials because you do not know which material counts and which material is extra. (For example, if there are four reading passages instead of three, three of the passages will count and one of the passages will not count. It is possible that the uncounted passage could be any of the four passages.)

REGISTRATION FOR THE TEST

It is important to understand the following information about registration for the TOEFL test:

- The first step in the registration process is to obtain a copy of the *TOEFL Information Bulletin*. This bulletin can be obtained by downloading it or ordering it from the TOEFL website at www.toefl.org.

- From the bulletin, it is possible to determine when and where the TOEFL iBT will be given.

- Procedures for completing the registration form and submitting it are listed in the *TOEFL Information Bulletin*. These procedures must be followed exactly.

HOW THE TEST IS SCORED

Students should keep the following information in mind about the scoring of the TOEFL iBT:

- The TOEFL iBT is scored on a scale of 0 to 120 points.

- Each of the four sections (Reading, Listening, Speaking, and Writing) receives a scaled score from 0 to 30. The scaled scores from the four sections are added together to determine the overall score.

- Speaking is initially given a score of 0 to 4, and writing is initially given a score of 0 to 5. These scores are converted to scaled scores of 0 to 30. Criteria for the 0 to 4 speaking scores are included on pages 101–102.

- After students complete the Speaking Pre-Test, Speaking Post-Test, Speaking Mini-Tests, and Speaking Complete Tests in the book, it is possible for them to estimate their scaled scores. A description of how to assess their speaking to determine approximate scaled scores of the various Speaking Tests is included on page 103.

- After students complete the Speaking Mini-Tests and Speaking Complete Tests on the CD-ROM, information allowing students to assess their speaking and determine approximate scaled scores is provided.

HOW iBT SCORES COMPARE WITH PAPER SCORES

Both versions of the TOEFL test (the PBT or Paper-Based Test and the iBT or Internet-Based Test) have different scaled score ranges. The paper TOEFL test has scaled scores ranging from 200 to 677; the iBT has scaled scores ranging from 0 to 120. The following chart shows how the scaled scores on the two versions of the TOEFL test are related:

iBT Internet-Based Test	PBT Paper-Based Test	iBT Internet-Based Test	PBT Paper-Based Test
120	677	65	513
115	650	60	497
110	637	55	480
105	620	50	463
100	600	45	450
95	587	40	433
90	577	35	417
85	563	30	397
80	550	25	377
75	537	20	350
70	523		

TO THE STUDENTS _____

HOW TO PREPARE FOR THE TOEFL iBT

The TOEFL iBT is a standardized test of English and academic skills. To do well on this test, you should therefore work in these areas to improve your score:

- You must work to improve your knowledge of the English *language skills* that are covered on the TOEFL iBT.
- You must work to improve your knowledge of the *academic skills* that are covered on the TOEFL iBT.
- You must understand the *test-taking strategies* that are appropriate for the TOEFL iBT.
- You must take *practice tests* with the focus of applying your knowledge of the appropriate language skills and test-taking strategies.

This book can familiarize you with the English language skills, academic skills, and test-taking strategies necessary for the Speaking section of the TOEFL iBT, and it can also provide you with a considerable amount of Speaking test practice. A huge amount of additional practice of the English language skills, academic skills, test-taking strategies, and tests for the Speaking section of the TOEFL iBT is found on the CD-ROM.

HOW TO USE THIS BOOK

This book provides a variety of materials to help you prepare for the Speaking section of the TOEFL iBT. Following these steps can help you to get the most out of this book:

1. Take the Speaking Diagnostic Pre-Test at the beginning of the book. When you take the Speaking Pre-Test, try to reproduce the conditions and time pressure of a real TOEFL test.
   a. Take each section of the test without interruption.
   b. Time yourself for each section so that you can experience the time pressure that exists on an actual TOEFL test.
   c. Play the listening audio one time only during the test. (You may play it more times when you are reviewing the test.)

2. After you complete the Speaking Diagnostic Pre-Test, you should assess and score it, and record your results.
   a. Complete the appropriate Skill-Assessment Checklists on pages 95–100 to assess the skills used in the test.
   b. Score your results using the Speaking Scoring Criteria on pages 101–102.
   c. Record your scores on the Test Results charts on pages 104–105.

3. Work through the presentations and exercises for the Speaking section, paying particular attention to the skills that caused you problems in the Speaking Diagnostic Pre-Test. Each time that you complete a TOEFL-format exercise, try to simulate the conditions and time pressure of a real TOEFL test. For speaking, allow yourself 15 to 20 seconds to prepare your response and 45 to 60 seconds to give your response.

4. When you have completed all the skills exercises for the Speaking section, take the Speaking Post-Test. Follow the directions above to reproduce the conditions and time pressure of a real TOEFL test. After you complete the Speaking Post-Test, follow the directions above to diagnose your answers and record your results.

5. As you work through the course material, periodically schedule Speaking Mini-Tests and Speaking Complete Tests. There are eight Speaking Mini-Tests and two Speaking Complete Tests in the book. As you take each of the tests, follow the directions above to reproduce the conditions and time pressure of a real TOEFL test. After you finish each test, follow the directions above to score it, diagnose your answers, and record your results.

HOW TO USE THE CD-ROM

The CD-ROM provides additional practice of the Speaking language skills and iBT-version Speaking tests to supplement the Speaking language skills and Speaking tests in the book. The material on the CD-ROM is completely different from the material in the book to provide the maximum amount of practice. You can now send your data and recordings from the CD-ROM to a server, and your teacher can receive this information in the form of a report. Following these steps can help you get the most out of the CD-ROM.

1. After you have completed the Speaking language skills in the book, you should complete the related Speaking Skills Practice exercises on the CD-ROM.

AFTER THIS IN THE BOOK	COMPLETE THIS ON THE CD-ROM
Independent Tasks (Skills 1–4)	Independent Tasks (Skills 1–4)
Integrated Tasks (Reading and Listening) (Skills 5–12)	Integrated Tasks (Reading and Listening) (Skills 5–12)
Integrated Tasks (Listening) (Skills 13–18)	Integrated Tasks (Listening) (Skills 13–18)

2. Work slowly and carefully through the Speaking Skills Practice exercises. These exercises are not timed but are instead designed to be done in a methodical and thoughtful way.

  a. Complete a Speaking task using the skills and strategies that you have learned in the book. Take good notes as you work on a task.

  b. Play back your spoken response.

  c. Use the *Sample Notes* button to compare your notes to the sample notes provided on the CD-ROM.

  d. Use the *Sample Answer* button to see an example of a good answer and to compare your response to this answer.

  e. Complete the *Skill-Assessment Checklist* to evaluate how well you completed your response.

3. As you work your way through the Skills Practice exercises, monitor your progress on the charts included in the program.

  a. The *Results Reports* include a list of each of the exercises that you have completed and how well you have done on each of the exercises. (If you do an exercise more than once, only the final attempt will be saved.) You can print the *Results Reports* if you would like to keep them in a notebook.

  b. The *Skills Reports* include a list of each of the language skills in the book, how many questions related to each language skill you have answered, and what percentage of the questions you have answered correctly. In this way, you can see clearly which language skills you have mastered and which language skills require further work. You can print the *Skills Reports* if you would like to keep them in a notebook.

4. Use the Speaking Mini-Tests and Speaking Complete Tests on the CD-ROM periodically throughout the course to determine how well you have learned to apply the language skills and test-taking strategies presented in the course. The CD-ROM includes eight Speaking Mini-Tests and two Speaking Complete Tests.

5. Take the tests in a manner that is as close as possible to the actual testing environment. Choose a time when you can work on a section without interruption.

6. Work straight through each test section. The *Sample Notes* and *Sample Answer* buttons are not available during test sections.

7. After you complete a Speaking test, do the following:
   a. Complete the *Skill-Assessment Checklist* as directed. (You must complete the *Skill-Assessment Checklist* to receive an estimated score.)
   b. Play back your spoken response.
   c. Use the *Sample Notes* button to compare your notes to the sample notes provided on the CD-ROM.
   d. Use the *Sample Answer* button to see an example of a good answer and to compare your response to this answer.

8. After you complete any tasks on the CD-ROM, send your data and recordings to your teacher. Click on SEND DATA from the Main Menu. Your teacher will provide you with a teacher's e-mail address and a class name to fill in.

TO THE TEACHER

HOW TO GET THE MOST OUT OF THE SKILLS EXERCISES IN THE BOOK

The skills exercises are a vital part of the TOEFL preparation process presented in this book. Maximum benefit can be obtained from the exercises if the students are properly prepared for the exercises and if the exercises are carefully reviewed after completion. Here are some suggestions:

• Be sure that the students have a clear idea of the appropriate skills and strategies involved in each exercise. Before beginning each exercise, review the skills and strategies that are used in that exercise. Then, when you review the exercises, reinforce the skills and strategies that can be used to determine the correct answers.

• As you review the exercises, be sure to discuss each answer and what makes it correct.

• The exercises are designed to be completed in class rather than assigned as homework. The exercises are short and take very little time to complete, particularly since it is important to keep students under time pressure while they are working on the exercises. Considerably more time should be spent in reviewing exercises than in actually doing them.

HOW TO GET THE MOST OUT OF THE TESTS IN THE BOOK

There are four different types of tests in this book: Speaking Diagnostic Pre-Test, Speaking Post-Test, Speaking Mini-Tests, and Speaking Complete Tests. When the tests are given, it is important that the test conditions be as similar to actual TOEFL test conditions as possible; each section of the test should be given without interruption and under the time pressure of the actual test. Giving the speaking tests in the book presents a unique problem because the students need to respond individually during the tests. Various ways of giving speaking tests are possible; you will need to determine the best way to give the speaking tests for your situation. Here are some suggestions:

- You can have the students come in individually and respond to the questions as the teacher listens to the responses and evaluates them.
- You can have a room set up where students come in individually to take a speaking test and record their responses on a cassette recorder. Then either the teacher or the student will need to evaluate the responses.
- You can have a room set up where students come in in groups of four to take a speaking test and record the responses on four cassette recorders, one in each corner of the room. Then either the teacher or the students will need to evaluate the responses.
- You can have the students sit down in an audio lab or computer lab where they can record their responses on the system or on cassette recorders. Then either the teacher or the students will need to evaluate the responses.

Review of the tests should emphasize the function served by each of these different types of tests:

- While reviewing the Speaking Diagnostic Pre-Test, you should encourage students to determine the areas where they require further practice.
- While reviewing the Speaking Post-Test, you should emphasize the language skills and strategies involved in determining the correct answer to each question.
- While reviewing the Speaking Mini-Tests, you should review the language skills and test-taking strategies that are applicable to the tests.
- While reviewing the Speaking Complete Tests, you should emphasize the overall strategies for the Speaking Complete Tests and review the variety of individual language skills and strategies taught throughout the course.

HOW TO GET THE MOST OUT OF THE CD-ROM

The CD-ROM is designed to supplement the practice that is contained in the book and to provide an alternate modality for preparation for the TOEFL iBT. Here are some ideas to consider as you decide how to incorporate the CD-ROM into your course:

- The CD-ROM is closely coordinated with the book and is intended to provide further practice of the skills and strategies that are presented in the book. This means that the overall organization of the CD-ROM parallels the organization of the book but that the exercise material and test items on the CD-ROM are different from those found in the book. It can thus be quite effective to teach and practice the language skills and strategies in the book and then use the CD-ROM for further practice and assignments.
- The CD-ROM can be used in a computer lab during class time (if you are lucky enough to have access to a computer lab during class time), but it does not need to be used in this way. It can also be quite effective to use the book during class time and to make assignments from the CD-ROM for the students to complete outside of class, either in the school computer lab or on their personal computers. Either method works quite well.
- The CD-ROM contains a Speaking Skills Practice section, eight Speaking Mini-Tests, and two Speaking Complete Tests. In the Speaking Skills Practice section, the students can practice and assess their mastery of specific skills. In the Speaking Mini-Tests and Speaking Complete Tests, the students can see how well they are able to apply their knowledge of the language skills and test-taking strategies to test sections.
- The CD-ROM scores the various Speaking tasks by counting the number of checkmarks on the Skill-Assessment Checklists. Scaled scores are assigned on the tests based on these checkmarks.

- The CD-ROM contains printable *Skills Reports* and *Results Reports* so that you can easily and efficiently keep track of your students' progress. You may want to ask your students to print the *Results Report* after they complete each exercise or test and compile the *Results Reports* in a notebook; you can then ask the students to turn in their notebooks periodically so that you can easily check that the assignments have been completed and monitor the progress that the students are making.

- The Speaking tasks can be reviewed by the students immediately after the students have completed them. Each Speaking task is also saved and can be accessed through the Results Menu, though only the most recent version of each Speaking task is saved. The Speaking tasks can also be saved to a disk and submitted to the teacher. (You could also have the students record their responses on a cassette recorder as they complete a test instead of having them record their responses on the computer. Then you could have the students turn in their cassettes for review instead of turning in computer disks.)

HOW MUCH TIME TO SPEND ON THE MATERIAL

You may have questions about how much time it takes to complete the materials in this course. The numbers in the following chart indicate approximately how many hours it takes to complete the material[1]:

BOOK		CD-ROM	
Speaking Pre-Test	2		
Speaking Skills 1–4	5	Speaking Skills 1–4	2
Speaking Skills 5–8	5	Speaking Skills 5–8	2
Speaking Skills 9–12	5	Speaking Skills 9–12	2
Speaking Skills 13–15	4	Speaking Skills 13–15	2
Speaking Skills 16–18	4	Speaking Skills 16–18	2
Speaking Post-Test	2		
Speaking Mini-Test 1	1	Speaking Mini-Test 1	1
Speaking Mini-Test 2	1	Speaking Mini-Test 2	1
Speaking Mini-Test 3	1	Speaking Mini-Test 3	1
Speaking Mini-Test 4	1	Speaking Mini-Test 4	1
Speaking Mini-Test 5	1	Speaking Mini-Test 5	1
Speaking Mini-Test 6	1	Speaking Mini-Test 6	1
Speaking Mini-Test 7	1	Speaking Mini-Test 7	1
Speaking Mini-Test 8	1	Speaking Mini-Test 8	1
Speaking Complete Test 1	2	Speaking Complete Test 1	2
Speaking Complete Test 2	2	Speaking Complete Test 2	2
	39 hours		**22 hours**

[1] The numbers related to the book indicate approximately how much class time it takes to introduce the material, complete the exercises, and review the exercises. The numbers related to the CD-ROM indicate approximately how much time it takes to complete the exercises and review them.

SPEAKING DIAGNOSTIC PRE-TEST

Speaking
Section Directions

This section tests your ability to speak about different topics. You will answer six questions. Answer each one as completely as you can.

Questions 1 and 2 will be about familiar topics. Try to speak about the topics clearly and coherently.

Questions 3 and 4 will include reading and listening. First, you will read a short passage. Then the text will disappear, and you will hear a talk about the same topic. Next you will answer a question about the text and the talk. Try to use information from the text and the talk to answer the question clearly and coherently to show that you understood the text and the talk.

Questions 5 and 6 will include part of a conversation or a lecture and a question. Try to answer the question clearly and coherently, using information from the conversation or lecture.

While you read and listen, you can take notes. You can use your notes to help you answer the questions.

Listen closely to the directions for each question. They will not appear on the screen.

Question 1

Read the question. On a piece of paper, take notes on the main points of a response. Then respond to the question.

What are the characteristics of a good teacher? Use reasons and examples to support your response.

Question 2

Read the question. On a piece of paper, take notes on the main points of a response. Then respond to the question.

Would you prefer to take a vacation in the mountains or at the ocean? Use reasons to support your response.

Question 3

Read the passage. On a piece of paper, take notes on the main points of the reading passage.

Notice from the Humanities Department

Because so many students have been registering for classes in the Humanities Department for which they have not fulfilled the prerequisites, the faculty committee of the Humanities Department has decided that a new policy will go into effect for the coming semester. This new policy, which was instituted by a unanimous vote of the faculty committee of the Humanities Department, is that all students who want to register in courses other than introductory courses in the Humanities Department must obtain signatures from their advisors before registering in these courses. It is the responsibility of advisors to determine if students have completed appropriate prerequisites before authorizing enrollment in courses.

Listen to the passage. On a piece of paper, take notes on the main points of the listening passage. 🎧

Now answer the following question:

How does the students' conversation add to the information included in the notice?

[Handwritten notes:]

a new policy
need advisor signature
to reg for any
class in humanities
class except introductory
courses.
• a topic
* From reading we
learned that ____
* from listening
we learned that ____

1. introduction: Topic of both reading and Listening.
2. Reading we can start with
3. listening → in the conversation we learned that
4. conclusion (sum up)

notice from hum. depart about Reg.
the dep reg adv. sign for admission
to all course exep introductory course
the man heard about the

Question 4

Read the passage. On a piece of paper, take notes on the main points of the reading passage.

Nonverbal communication is any kind of communication that takes place without the use of words. It can refer to facial expressions such as smiling or frowning; it can refer to movements of the head such as nodding the head to show agreement or shaking it to show disagreement; it can refer to hand gestures such as offering the hand to shake in greeting or waving the hand to say "hello" or "good-bye." Nonverbal communication can also refer to a whole host of other ways of communicating without words inasmuch as nonverbal communication is limited only by exclusion: it is any type of communication *without* words. Communication is verbal if words are used; it is nonverbal if words are not used.

Listen to the passage. On a piece of paper, take notes on the main points of the listening passage. 🎧

[handwritten notes: any comm without words / facial exp. / head movement / hand gestures]

Now answer the following question:

How does the professor supplement the information included in the reading?

[handwritten notes: → non-verbal communication — doesn't require intended. → doesn't take place if other doesn't understand. Topic: non verbal communication Reading we learn in met]

This Listening is a conversation b/w 2 student.
Female & Male students, the q student is having a problem
with her French level class, the male student

Question 5

Listen to the passage. On a piece of paper, take notes on the main points of the listening passage. 🎧

Suggest to ask friends & professor.

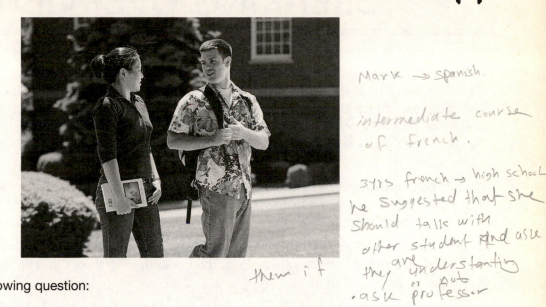

Mark → spanish.

intermediate course of french.

3yrs french → high school
he suggested that she should talk with other student and ask them if they are understanding or not
• ask professor if she is not the right level

Now answer the following question:

What does the man suggest the woman should do to deal with the problem she is having?

Question 6

Listen to the passage. On a piece of paper, take notes on the main points of the listening passage. 🎧

• Serier & clicks that sond by whales & reflect to whales.
• can learn size & shape of object
• & how far it

whales how use echolcation
Technigue to find what happened to surrounded

Echo

• 2 whales
• tooth whales can use echolvratin.

Now answer the following question:

they are moving

What points does the professor make about echolocation?

how fast & what direction. & movement.

Turn to pages 94–105 to *assess* the skills used in the test,
score the test using the Speaking Scoring Criteria, and *record* your results.

In this listening the professor discussed whales & echo
which is technig used by whales to know more about the surround. only tooth

SPEAKING OVERVIEW

The third section on the TOEFL iBT is the Speaking section. This section consists of six tasks: two independent tasks and four integrated tasks. Two of the integrated tasks combine reading and listening with speaking, and the other two integrated tasks combine listening with speaking. To complete these tasks, you will speak into a microphone and your responses will be recorded on the computer.

- The two **independent** tasks each consist of a question to be answered. The ideas in your responses come from your personal experience rather than from material that is given to you.

- The two **reading, listening, and speaking integrated** tasks each consist of a reading passage, a listening passage, and a question that asks how the ideas in the two passages are related.

- The two **listening and speaking integrated** tasks each consist of a longer listening passage and a question that asks you to summarize key points of the passage.

Because these kinds of tasks are different, there are different strategies for each kind. The following strategies can help you on the independent tasks in the Speaking section.

STRATEGIES FOR AN INDEPENDENT SPEAKING TASK

1. **Be familiar with the directions.** The directions on every test are the same, so it is not necessary to spend time reading the directions carefully when you take the test. You should be completely familiar with the directions before the day of the test.

2. **Dismiss the directions as soon as they come up.** You should already be familiar with the directions, so you can click on Continue as soon as it appears and use your time on the passages and questions.

3. **Read the question carefully, and answer the question exactly as it is asked.** You will be given some time at the beginning of the task to be sure that you understand the question and what the question is asking you to do.

4. **Organize your response very clearly.** You should have an introduction, supporting details, and perhaps a conclusion.

5. **Use transitions to make your response cohesive.** Your response is easier to understand if you show how the ideas in your response are related.

6. **Stick to vocabulary, sentence structures, and grammatical points that you know.** This is not the best time to try out new words, structures, or grammar points.

7. **Speak slowly and distinctly.** It is better to speak clearly so that you can be understood than to race through your response so that you will be able to say more.

8. **Monitor the time carefully on the title bar of the computer screen.** The title bar indicates how much time you have to complete your response.

The following strategies can help you on the reading, listening, and speaking integrated tasks in the Speaking section.

STRATEGIES FOR AN INTEGRATED SPEAKING TASK
(Reading, Listening, and Speaking)

1. **Be familiar with the directions.** The directions on every test are the same, so it is not necessary to spend time reading the directions carefully when you take the test. You should be completely familiar with the directions before the day of the test.

2. **Dismiss the directions as soon as they come up.** You should already be familiar with the directions, so you can click on ⬜ Continue ⬜ as soon as it appears and use your time on the passages and questions.

3. **Do not worry if the material in the integrated task is on a topic that is not familiar to you.** All of the information that you need to plan your response is included in the passages. You do not need any background knowledge to answer the questions.

4. **Read the reading passage carefully.** You will have only a limited time to read the passage.

5. **Take careful notes as you read the passage.** You should focus on the main points and key supporting material. Do not try to write down everything you read. Do not write down too many unnecessary details.

6. **Listen carefully to the passage.** You will hear the passage one time only. You may not hear the passage again.

7. **Take careful notes as you listen to the spoken material.** You should focus on the main points and key supporting material. Do not try to write down everything you hear. Do not write down too many unnecessary details.

8. **Organize your response very clearly.** You should have an overall topic statement that shows the relationship between the reading passage and the listening passage. You should also discuss the reading passage and the listening passage.

9. **Use transitions to make your response cohesive.** Your response is easier to understand if you show how the ideas in your response are related.

10. **Stick to vocabulary, sentence structures, and grammatical points that you know.** This is not the best time to try out new words, structures, or grammar points.

11. **Speak slowly and distinctly.** It is better to speak clearly so that you can be understood than to race through your response so that you can say more.

12. **Monitor the time carefully on the title bar of the computer screen.** The title bar indicates how much time you have to complete your response.

The following strategies can help you on the listening and speaking integrated tasks in the Speaking section.

STRATEGIES FOR AN INTEGRATED SPEAKING TASK
(Listening and Speaking)

---

1. **Be familiar with the directions.** The directions on every test are the same, so it is not necessary to spend time reading the directions carefully when you take the test. You should be completely familiar with the directions before the day of the test.

2. **Dismiss the directions as soon as they come up.** You should already be familiar with the directions, so you can click on Continue as soon as it appears and use your time on the passages and questions.

3. **Do not worry if the material in the integrated task is on a topic that is not familiar to you.** All of the information that you need to plan your response is included in the passages. You do not need any background knowledge to answer the questions.

4. **Listen carefully to the passage.** You will hear the passage one time only. You may not hear the passage again.

5. **Take careful notes as you listen to the spoken material.** You should focus on the main points and key supporting material. Do not try to write down everything you hear. Do not write down too many unnecessary details.

6. **Organize your response very clearly.** You should have an overall topic statement that states the main point of the passage and details that support the main point.

7. **Use transitions to make your response cohesive.** Your response is easier to understand if you show how the ideas in your response are related.

8. **Stick to vocabulary, sentence structures, and grammatical points that you know.** This is not the best time to try out new words, structures, or grammar points.

9. **Speak slowly and distinctly.** It is better to speak clearly so that you can be understood than to race through your response so that you can say more.

10. **Monitor the time carefully on the title bar of the computer screen.** The title bar indicates how much time you have to complete your response.

SPEAKING SKILLS

The following skills will help you to implement these strategies in the Speaking section of the TOEFL iBT.

INDEPENDENT TASKS

There are two independent speaking tasks. These two independent speaking tasks are a free-choice response and a paired-choice response.

Speaking Skill 1: PLAN THE FREE-CHOICE RESPONSE

The first and most important step in the independent free-choice task in the Speaking section of the TOEFL iBT is to decode the question to determine what the intended outline is. Independent free-choice questions generally give clear clues about how your answer should be constructed. It is important to follow the clues that are given in the topic when you are planning your answer. You will probably not be given too much credit for a response that does not cover the question in the way that is intended. Study the following question.

> **Question**
>
> Where would you like to be professionally in ten years? Use details to support your response.

As you read this topic, you should quickly determine that you should state clearly *where you would like to be professionally in ten years* and support that statement with *details*. You will have a little bit of time before you speak to plan your ideas. Study the following plan for the response to the question.

INTRODUCTION:	I would like to own my own business
SUPPORTING IDEA 1:	first step
	will get master's in business
	(entrepreneurship)
SUPPORTING IDEA 2:	second step
	will work in company while planning my
	business
SUPPORTING IDEA 3:	third step
	will start my own business when I am ready
CONCLUSION:	I can succeed by following this process.

In this plan, there is an introduction about owning my own business and supporting details about the steps I will take to work toward this goal. There is also a conclusion that I can succeed by following this process.

The following chart outlines the key information that you should remember about planning the response.

PLANNING THE RESPONSE	
QUESTION	Each question in the independent free-choice task shows you *what* you should discuss and *how* you should organize your response. You must decode the question to determine how to organize your response.
INTRODUCTION	Begin your response with an introduction.
SUPPORTING IDEAS	Support your introduction with the kinds of ideas that the question asks for (such as reasons, details, or examples).
CONCLUSION	If you have time, end with a conclusion that restates the main point in your introduction.

SPEAKING EXERCISE 1: For each of the following questions, prepare a plan that shows the type of information you will include in your response.

1.
> What are the characteristics of a good neighbor? Use reasons and details to support your response.

INTRODUCTION: The two most important characteristics are friendliness and helpfulness

SUPPORTING IDEA 1: first reason
friendliness because I want to live in a place where people are friendly

SUPPORTING IDEA 2: second reason
helpfulness because it is important for neighbors to help in times of need

CONCLUSION: Friendliness and helpfulness are important characteristics.

2.
> What is your favorite holiday? Use reasons and details to support your response.

INTRODUCTION:

SUPPORTING IDEA 1:

SUPPORTING IDEA 2:

CONCLUSION:

3. Which person has helped you the most to get where you are today, and how has he or she helped you? Use examples to support your response.

INTRODUCTION:

SUPPORTING IDEA 1:

SUPPORTING IDEA 2:

CONCLUSION:

4. If you suddenly got $10 million, what would you spend it on? Use details to support your response.

INTRODUCTION:

SUPPORTING IDEA 1:

SUPPORTING IDEA 2:

CONCLUSION:

5. What does your dream house look like? Use details to support your response.

INTRODUCTION:

SUPPORTING IDEA 1:

SUPPORTING IDEA 2:

CONCLUSION:

6. What is your favorite food? Use reasons and details to support your response.

INTRODUCTION:

SUPPORTING IDEA 1:

SUPPORTING IDEA 2:

CONCLUSION:

7. What are the characteristics of a good parent? Use reasons and details to support your response.

INTRODUCTION:

SUPPORTING IDEA 1:

SUPPORTING IDEA 2:

CONCLUSION:

8. If you could live anywhere, where would you live? Use reasons to support your response.

INTRODUCTION:

SUPPORTING IDEA 1:

SUPPORTING IDEA 2:

CONCLUSION:

9. What person who is alive today would you most like to meet? Use reasons and details to support your response.

INTRODUCTION:

SUPPORTING IDEA 1:

SUPPORTING IDEA 2:

CONCLUSION:

10. Why are you preparing to take the TOEFL test? Use reasons to support your response.

INTRODUCTION:

SUPPORTING IDEA 1:

SUPPORTING IDEA 2:

CONCLUSION:

Speaking Skill 2: MAKE THE FREE-CHOICE RESPONSE

After you have planned your response, you need to make your response. As you make your response, you should think about the following four things: (1) you should start with an introduction, (2) you should support the introduction, (3) you should use transitions to show how the ideas are related, and (4) you should end with a conclusion.

Look at the plan for a response to the independent speaking task on where you would like to be in ten years and a sample response based on these notes.

INTRODUCTION: I would like to own my own business

SUPPORTING IDEA 1: first step
will get master's in business (entrepreneurship)

SUPPORTING IDEA 2: second step
will work in company while planning my business

SUPPORTING IDEA 3: third step
will start my own business when I am ready

CONCLUSION: I can succeed by following this process.

In ten years, I would like to own an import business of my own. Next year, I will be starting a master's program in business with a specialization in entrepreneurship. I will be getting this degree because I hope to start my own business and make it successful some day. After I finish my master's degree three years from now, I will most likely take a position in another company for a few years to make some money and to spend some time planning my own business. Within ten years, I hope to own my own company and be on the way to making it a success. If I follow this process, I know I can succeed.

You should notice that this response includes an introduction followed by several supporting details. The transitions *in ten years, next year, three years from now,* and *within ten years* are used to show how the ideas are related. The response ends with a conclusion.

The following chart outlines the key information you should remember about making the response.

MAKING THE RESPONSE	
INTRODUCTION	Start your response with an introduction that states the topic and your main point about the topic.
SUPPORT	Include details to support the introduction.
TRANSITIONS	Use *transitions* to show how the ideas in the response are related.
CONCLUSION	End your response with a conclusion that restates the main point.

SPEAKING EXERCISE 2: Create responses for the independent speaking tasks that you have been working on in Speaking Skills 1–2.

SPEAKING REVIEW EXERCISE (Skills 1–2): Read each question. On a piece of paper, take notes on the main points of each response. Then respond to each question.

1. If you could have any job in the world, what would it be? Use details to support your response.

2. At what age should a person be allowed to drive? Use reasons to support your response.

3. What is the best excuse to give your teacher when you have not done the homework? Use reasons to support your response.

4. What is your favorite day of the year? Use reasons to support your response.

5. What change would you like your government to make? Use reasons to support your response.

Speaking Skill 3: PLAN THE PAIRED-CHOICE RESPONSE

The first and most important step in the independent paired-choice task in the Speaking section of the TOEFL iBT is to decode the question to determine what the intended outline is. Independent paired-choice questions generally give clear clues about how your answer should be constructed. It is important to follow the clues that are given in the topic when you are planning your answer. You will probably not be given too much credit for a response that does not cover the question in the way that is intended. Study the following question.

Question

Do you like to try new kinds of food or eat the same kind of food all the time? Use details and examples to support your response.

As you read this topic, you should quickly determine that you should state clearly whether *you like to try new kinds of food or eat the same kind of food* and support that statement with *details and examples*. You will have a little bit of time before you speak to plan your ideas. Study the following plan for the response to the question.

INTRODUCTION:	I think I am the kind of person who tries new food, but I am not
SUPPORTING IDEA 1:	first reason I like to meet new people, go to new places, try new things
SUPPORTING IDEA 2:	second reason I don't like to try new food
SUPPORTING IDEA 3:	example time last week when I went to new restaurant but didn't try new food
CONCLUSION:	I am not really adventurous with food.

In this plan, there is an introduction about the kind of person I am and supporting details and an example about what I really like. There is a conclusion about not being adventurous with food.

The following chart outlines the key information that you should remember about planning the response.

PLANNING THE RESPONSE	
QUESTION	Each question in the independent paired-choice task shows you *what* you should discuss and *how* you should organize your response. You must decode the question to determine how to organize your response.
INTRODUCTION	Begin your response with an introduction.
SUPPORTING IDEAS	Support your introduction with the kinds of ideas that the question asks for (such as reasons, details, or examples).
CONCLUSION	If you have time, end with a conclusion that restates the main point in the introduction.

SPEAKING EXERCISE 3: For each of the following questions, prepare a plan that shows the type of information you will include in your response.

1.
> Do you prefer to be in a large or a small class? Use reasons to support your response.

INTRODUCTION: I think it is better to be in a large class

SUPPORTING IDEA 1:   <u>first reason</u>
                      hear ideas from many rather than from few

SUPPORTING IDEA 2:   <u>second reason</u>
                      one student can't dominate larger class

CONCLUSION: For these reasons, it is better to be in a large class.

2.
> Would you prefer to go out to dinner or stay home and cook a meal? Use reasons to support your response.

INTRODUCTION:

SUPPORTING IDEA 1:

SUPPORTING IDEA 2:

CONCLUSION:

3.
> Do you think it is better to marry before or after the age of thirty? Use reasons to support your response.

INTRODUCTION:

SUPPORTING IDEA 1:

SUPPORTING IDEA 2:

CONCLUSION:

4. Do you prefer to take essay exams or multiple-choice exams? Use reasons to support your response.

INTRODUCTION:

SUPPORTING IDEA 1:

SUPPORTING IDEA 2:

CONCLUSION:

5. Would you prefer to take a trip by plane or by train? Use reasons to support your response.

INTRODUCTION:

SUPPORTING IDEA 1:

SUPPORTING IDEA 2:

CONCLUSION:

6. Would you like to live in a big city or a small town? Use reasons to support your response.

INTRODUCTION:

SUPPORTING IDEA 1:

SUPPORTING IDEA 2:

CONCLUSION:

7. Do you think it is better to study alone or study with friends? Use reasons to support your response.

INTRODUCTION:

SUPPORTING IDEA 1:

SUPPORTING IDEA 2:

CONCLUSION:

8. Do you prefer to play sports or watch sports? Use reasons to support your response.

INTRODUCTION:

SUPPORTING IDEA 1:

SUPPORTING IDEA 2:

CONCLUSION:

9. Would you prefer to go to the opera or to a football game? Use reasons and details to support your response.

INTRODUCTION:

SUPPORTING IDEA 1:

SUPPORTING IDEA 2:

CONCLUSION:

10. Would you prefer to take the TOEFL test or a math test? Use reasons and details to support your response.

INTRODUCTION:

SUPPORTING IDEA 1:

SUPPORTING IDEA 2:

CONCLUSION:

Speaking Skill 4: MAKE THE PAIRED-CHOICE RESPONSE

After you have planned your response, you need to make your response. As you make your response, you should think about the following four things: (1) you should start with an introduction, (2) you should support the introduction, (3) you should use transitions to show how the ideas are related, and (4) you should end with a conclusion.

Look at the plan for a response to the independent speaking task on whether you like to try new foods or not and a sample response based on these notes.

INTRODUCTION:	I think I am the kind of person who tries new food, but I am not
SUPPORTING IDEA 1:	<u>first reason</u> I like to meet new people, go to new places, try new things
SUPPORTING IDEA 2:	<u>second reason</u> I don't like to try new food
SUPPORTING IDEA 3:	<u>example</u> time last week when I went to new restaurant but didn't try new food
CONCLUSION:	I am not really adventurous with food.

I like to think that I'm the kind of person who is willing to try new kinds of food, but when I get right down to it, it seems that I'm not that adventurous when it comes to trying new kinds of food. I think of myself as an adventurous person; I like to meet new people, go to new places, and try new things. However, whenever I'm given the choice of trying new food or sticking with the regular food I'm familiar with, I seem to avoid new kinds of food. Last week, for instance, my friends wanted to try a new restaurant, and they ordered new things while I ordered the same old hamburger and fries. You can see from this that I am not really adventurous with food.

You should notice that this response includes an introduction followed by several supporting details. The transitions *however* and *for instance* are used to show how the ideas are related. It ends with a conclusion.

The following chart outlines the key information you should remember about making the response.

MAKING THE RESPONSE	
INTRODUCTION	Start your response with an *introduction* that states the topic and your main point about the topic.
SUPPORT	Include *details* to support the introduction.
TRANSITIONS	Use *transitions* to show how ideas in the response are related.
CONCLUSION	End your response with a conclusion that restates the main point.

SPEAKING EXERCISE 4: Create responses for the independent speaking tasks that you have been working on in Speaking Skills 3–4.

SPEAKING REVIEW EXERCISE (Skills 3–4): Read each question. On a piece of paper, take notes on the main points of each response. Then respond to each question.

1. If your teacher makes a mistake, is it better to correct the teacher or ignore the mistake? Use reasons to support your response.

2. Is it better to take chances in life or play it safe?

3. Is it better to have a career that pays a lot of money but keeps you away from your family or a career that does not pay so much but allows you time with your family? Use reasons to support your response.

4. Do you make decisions quickly or take your time making them? Use details and examples to support your response.

5. Do you think children should always obey their parents, or are there times when it is not necessary for children to obey?

INTEGRATED TASKS (Reading and Listening) _____

There are two integrated tasks that integrate speaking with reading and listening. These two integrated speaking tasks are on a campus topic and on an academic topic.

Speaking Skill 5: NOTE THE MAIN POINTS AS YOU READ

In the first reading, listening, and speaking integrated task in the Speaking section of the TOEFL iBT, you will be asked to read a passage from a campus setting as part of the task. In this part of the integrated task, it is important for you to be able to read a campus passage of 100–120 words and take notes on the main points of the reading passage in a short period of time. Look at the following example of a reading passage that is part of an integrated speaking task.

Reading Passage

A notice from the office of the university president

The university president would like to make sure that it is perfectly clear to all university professors, administrators, students, and any other members of the university community that university policy requires that no pets be allowed on campus. The only exception to this rule, absolutely the only exception, is animals such as seeing-eye dogs that are trained for use in assisting persons with disabilities. Any other pets, no matter how large or small, are unequivocally not allowed. Anyone who fails to follow this policy, be they faculty, administrators, students, or others, will face immediate action by the university.

As you read the passage, you should take notes on the topic and main points of the reading passage. Look at these notes on the topic and main points of the reading passage.

TOPIC OF READING PASSAGE: notice from university president on policy against pets on campus

main points about the notice:
- reminds university community about policy against pets on campus (except animals for persons with disabilities)
- tells campus community that action will be taken against anyone with pets on campus

---

These notes show that the topic of the reading passage is a *notice from the university president on a policy against pets on campus*; the main points about the notice are that it *reminds the university community about* the existing *policy against pets on campus except for animals* used by people *with disabilities* and that it *tells the campus community that action will be taken against anyone with pets on campus.*

The following chart outlines the key information you should remember about dealing with the reading passage in the reading, listening, and speaking integrated speaking task.

NOTING THE MAIN POINTS IN THE READING PASSAGE	
TOPIC	Make sure that you understand (and take notes on) the *topic* of the reading passage.
MAIN POINTS	Then focus on (and take notes on) the *main points* that are used to support the topic of the reading passage.

SPEAKING EXERCISE 5: Read each of the following passages, and note the *topic* and the *main points* that are used to support the topic.

1. Read the passage. Take notes on the main points of the reading passage.

A notice from campus administration

This campus has a serious problem with bicycles: too many students are parking their bicycles in unauthorized places. Beginning on Monday, November 1, any bicycles left in unauthorized places will be ticketed. Please note that there is authorized parking for bicycles along the east and west sides of campus. Parking of bicycles is allowed only in places where signs are posted indicating that bicycle parking is allowed. In places where no signs are posted, bicycle parking is not allowed.

TOPIC OF READING PASSAGE:

main points about the topic:

-

-

2. Read the passage. Take notes on the main points of the reading passage.

A message from the university president

It is with a sense of both joy and regret that the university announces the retirement of Dr. Margaret Connor, who has been something of an institution at this university for almost half a century. Dr. Connor will be retiring at the end of the spring semester next year, at which time she will have completed fifty years of service to the university. Dr. Connor came to this university as a graduate student, and then, after completing her doctorate in psychology, she became a professor in the Psychology Department. She has been praised for her commitment to her students over the decades and has published articles and books too numerous to mention. Though she will certainly be missed by the university community, we all wish her well in her retirement.

TOPIC OF READING PASSAGE:

main points about the topic:

-

-

3. Read the passage. Take notes on the main points of the reading passage.

A part of a class syllabus

Just a word of warning to all of you. I have listed the assignments and the dates they are due here for you, so please pay attention to them. I do not accept late assignments, ever. On the date that an assignment is due, it is your responsibility to get it in on time. No excuses will be accepted, not even serious illness or injury. My strong advice to you is that you get your assignments done early so that you will be able to turn them in on time even if something serious comes up. Your grade on any assignment that is turned in late will be zero, so if you do not get an assignment done on time, do not bother to turn it in late.

TOPIC OF READING PASSAGE:

<u>main points about the topic:</u>

-

-

Speaking Skill 6: NOTE THE MAIN POINTS AS YOU LISTEN

In the first reading, listening, and speaking integrated task in the Speaking section of the TOEFL iBT, you will also be asked to listen to a passage from a campus situation as part of the task. In this part of the integrated task, it is important for you to be able to listen to a campus passage of 1–2 minutes and take notes on the main points of the listening passage as you listen. Look at the following example of a listening passage that is part of the integrated speaking task.

Listening Passage

(woman)   *You saw the notice from the university president?*
(man)   *I certainly did.*
(woman)   *From the tone of the notice, it sounded as if he was kind of upset, don't you think?*
(man)   *I do.*
(woman)   *I wonder why he created this new policy.*
(man)   *Well, it wasn't a new policy. . . . He was just reminding us of a policy that already existed. . . . But, you didn't hear why he put out this notice reminding us about the policy?*
(woman)   *No, I didn't. Did you?*
(man)   *Well, I heard something. This is what some of the other guys told me. They said that one of the professors in the Biology Department has a pet snake.*
(woman)   *A pet snake?*
(man)   *Yeah, a really big one. Anyway, the snake got out somehow, it escaped, and got into the president's office somehow.*
(woman)   *Oh, no!*
(man)   *Yeah, the president got quite a surprise when he sat down at his desk and felt this snake under his desk.*
(woman)   *Okay. Now I see why the president issued the notice.*

As you listen to the passage, you should take notes on the topic and main points of the listening passage. Look at these notes on the topic and main points of the listening passage.

> TOPIC OF LISTENING PASSAGE: why the president issued the notice
>
> reasons for issuing the notice:
> - policy against pets on campus already existed
> - professor in Biology Department had pet snake anyway
> - snake escaped and got into president's office
> - president wanted to remind campus of existing policy

These notes show that the topic of the listening passage is *why the president issued the notice,* and the details to explain why the notice was issued are that there was already a *policy against pets on campus,* that a *professor in the Biology Department had a pet snake* in spite of the policy, that the pet *snake escaped and got into the president's office,* and that the *president wanted to remind the campus* that there already was a policy against having pets on campus.

The following chart outlines the key information you should remember about dealing with the listening passage in the reading, listening, and speaking integrated speaking task.

NOTING THE MAIN POINTS IN THE LISTENING PASSAGE	
TOPIC	Make sure that you understand (and take notes on) the *topic* of the listening passage.
MAIN POINTS	Then focus on (and take notes on) the *main points* that are used to support the topic of the listening passage.

SPEAKING EXERCISE 6: Listen to each of the following passages, and note the *topic* and the *main points* that are used to support the topic.

1. Listen to the passage. Take notes on the main points of the listening passage. 🎧

TOPIC OF LISTENING PASSAGE:

main points about the topic:

-
-

2. Listen to the passage. Take notes on the main points of the listening passage. 🎧

TOPIC OF LISTENING PASSAGE:

main points about the topic:

-
-

3. Listen to the passage. Take notes on the main points of the listening passage. 🎧

TOPIC OF LISTENING PASSAGE:

main points about the topic:

-

-

Speaking Skill 7: PLAN BEFORE YOU SPEAK

After you have noted the main points of the reading passage and the main points of the listening passage in the campus integrated reading, listening, and speaking task, you need to read the question and plan your response.

The question will most likely be about how the main points of the reading passage and the main points of the listening passage are related. Look at the following example of a question in a reading, listening, and speaking integrated speaking task on the notice about the university policy on pets.

Question

How does the information in the students' conversation add to the information in the notice on the university's policy on pets?

You can see that, although the question does not specifically mention "main points" of the reading passage and listening passage, the question is in reality asking you to show how the main points of these two passages are related.

To prepare a plan for your response, you should look at the notes you have taken on the reading passage and the notes you have taken on the listening passage and focus on how the ideas in the two passages are related. Look at the following plan for a response to the integrated speaking task on the university's policy on pets.

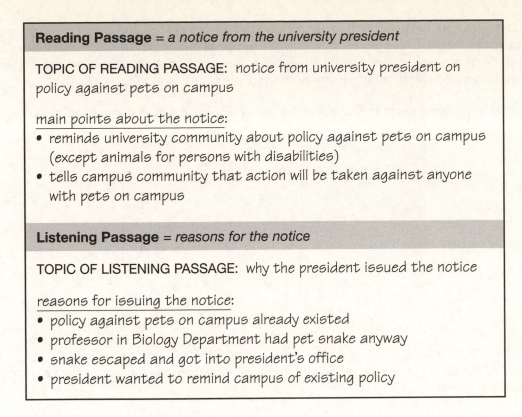

Reading Passage = *a notice from the university president*

TOPIC OF READING PASSAGE: notice from university president on policy against pets on campus

main points about the notice:
- reminds university community about policy against pets on campus (except animals for persons with disabilities)
- tells campus community that action will be taken against anyone with pets on campus

Listening Passage = *reasons for the notice*

TOPIC OF LISTENING PASSAGE: why the president issued the notice

reasons for issuing the notice:
- policy against pets on campus already existed
- professor in Biology Department had pet snake anyway
- snake escaped and got into president's office
- president wanted to remind campus of existing policy

From this plan, you can see the way that the ideas in the reading passage and the listening passage are related. The plan shows that the reading passage describes *a notice from the university president* and the listening passage provides *the reasons for the notice*.

The following chart outlines the key information you should remember about planning before you speak in a reading, listening, and speaking integrated speaking task.

PLANNING BEFORE YOU SPEAK	
QUESTION	Study the *question* to determine what is being asked. Expect that the question is asking how the ideas in the reading passage and the listening passage are related.
RELATIONSHIP	Look at the notes you have taken on the reading passage and the listening passage, and focus on the main points or topics of each passage. Then describe how the ideas in each of the two passages are *related*.

SPEAKING EXERCISE 7: Look at the notes that you prepared for the reading passages in Speaking Exercise 5 and the listening passages in Speaking Exercise 6. Read the question for each task. Then prepare a plan for your response. Be sure to note the relationship between the reading passage and the listening passage in your plan.

1. How do the students seem to feel about the notice on bicycles from campus administration?

2. How does the students' conversation add to the information in the message about a certain university professor?

3. What is the students' reaction to the information in the syllabus that is presented in the reading passage?

Speaking Skill 8: MAKE THE RESPONSE

After you have planned your response, you need to make your response. As you make your response, you should think about the following three things: (1) you should start with a topic statement, (2) you should support the topic statement, and (3) you should use transitions to show how the ideas are related.

Look at the plan for a response on the integrated speaking task on the university's policy on pets and a sample response based on these notes.

Reading Passage = *a notice from the university president*

TOPIC OF READING PASSAGE: notice from university president on policy against pets on campus

main points about the notice:
- reminds university community about policy against pets on campus (except animals for persons with disabilities)
- tells campus community that action will be taken against anyone with pets on campus

Listening Passage = *reasons for the notice*

TOPIC OF LISTENING PASSAGE: why the president issued the notice

reasons for issuing the notice:
- policy against pets on campus already existed
- professor in Biology Department had pet snake anyway
- snake escaped and got into president's office
- president wanted to remind campus of existing policy

In this set of materials, the reading passage describes a notice from the university president, and the listening passage provides a student discussion of the reasons for the notice.

The notice that is described in the reading passage reminds the university community about a policy against pets on campus, except for animals for persons with disabilities. The notice (also) tells the university community that action will be taken against anyone with pets on campus.

In the listening passage, the students discuss the reasons why this notice was issued. The students say that a policy against pets already existed on campus. (However,) a professor in the Biology Department had a pet snake anyway, and the pet snake escaped and got into the president's office. The president most likely issued the notice to remind the campus of the existing policy.

You should notice that this response begins with a topic statement showing the relationship between the information in the reading passage and the listening passage. Two supporting paragraphs follow the topic statement, describing the main points of the reading passage and the listening passage. The transitions *also* and *however* are used to show how the ideas in the supporting paragraphs are related.

The following chart outlines the key information you should remember about making the response.

MAKING THE RESPONSE	
TOPIC	Start your response with a *topic statement* that shows how the ideas in the reading passage and the ideas in the listening passage are related.
SUPPORT	Include the *key points* of the reading passage and the listening passage in your response.
TRANSITIONS	Use *transitions* to show how the ideas are related.

SPEAKING EXERCISE 8: Create responses for the integrated reading, listening, and speaking tasks that you have been working on in Speaking Skills 5–8.

SPEAKING REVIEW EXERCISE (Skills 5–8):
Read the passage. On a piece of paper, take notes on the main points of the reading passage.

Part of the syllabus in a history class

The research paper is worth 40 percent of your grade. What you are to do is choose an event from history and research that event and then write a paper on the results of your research. However, I want you to do something a bit different from a typical research paper. I want you to write about the event from two perspectives, one positive and one negative. What you will find, in the study of history, is that a single event can be described in two very different ways. Thus, for your assignment, I want you to research a particular person or event from two perspectives, one positive and one negative.

Listen to the passage. On a piece of paper, take notes on the main points of the listening passage.

Now answer the following question:

How does the information in the listening passage add to the information in the reading passage?

Speaking Skill 9: NOTE THE MAIN POINTS AS YOU READ

In the second reading, listening, and speaking integrated task in the Speaking section of the TOEFL iBT, you will be asked to read an academic passage as part of the task. In this part of the integrated task, it is important for you to be able to read an academic passage of 100–120 words and take notes on the main points of the reading passage in a short period of time. Look at the following example of a reading passage that is part of an integrated speaking task on the author Isaac Asimov.

Reading Passage

Isaac Asimov

Isaac Asimov (1920–1992) was an amazing author who wrote an astounding amount of material on an even more astounding variety of subjects. His literary studies included line-by-line analyses of all of the plays of Shakespeare; his historical research included works on the history of Greece, the Roman Empire, England, and France; he also wrote well-researched tomes on physics, chemistry, and astronomy. What he is most likely best known for today, however, is science fiction: his *Foundation* series on a galactic empire inspired by Gibbon's *Decline and Fall of the Roman Empire* and the *I, Robot* series about a future society where humans and robots coexist. In total, Asimov wrote more than 500 books on this wide variety of subjects.

As you read the passage, you should take notes on the topic and main points of the reading passage. Look at these notes on the topic and main points of the reading passage.

TOPIC OF READING PASSAGE: author Isaac Asimov

main points about Asimov:
• wrote a huge amount of material (more than 500 books)
• wrote on a wide variety of topics (literary analysis, history, physics, chemistry, astronomy, science fiction)

These notes show that the topic of the reading passage is the *author Isaac Asimov*; the main points about Asimov are that he *wrote a huge amount of material (more than 500 books)* and that he *wrote on a wide variety of topics* including *literary analysis, history, physics, chemistry, astronomy,* and *science fiction.*

The following chart outlines the key information you should remember about dealing with the reading passage in the integrated speaking task.

NOTING THE MAIN POINTS IN THE READING PASSAGE	
TOPIC	Make sure that you understand (and take notes on) the *topic* of the reading passage.
MAIN POINTS	Then focus on (and take notes on) the *main points* that are used to support the topic of the reading passage.

SPEAKING EXERCISE 9: Read each of the following passages, and note the *topic* and the *main points* that are used to support the topic.

1. Read the passage. Take notes on the main points of the reading passage.

The Dead Sea

The Middle Eastern body of water called *Bahr Lut* in Arabic is known as the Dead Sea in English. This body of water is said to be "dead" not because it is the dried-out remnant of a formerly living sea but instead because its high salinity makes it difficult for life-forms to survive in it. The Dead Sea is a landlocked body of water with the Jordan River as its source and no outlet. Its high salt content, which results from the rapid evaporation due to the area's extremely high temperatures, makes it the saltiest body of water on Earth.

TOPIC OF READING PASSAGE:

main points about the topic:

-

-

2. Read the passage. Take notes on the main points of the reading passage.

Polling

Polling is, of course, a survey of certain people to find out how they feel about an issue or about a candidate for a government post in an election. Polling involves, simply, asking people how they feel about an issue or a person and then tallying the results. When it is not feasible to contact everyone involved to find out what each person thinks because there are, for example, too many people to contact each one individually, then a representative sample of people can be polled and the results of the representative sample can be attributed to the population as a whole.

TOPIC OF READING PASSAGE:

main points about the topic:

-

-

3. Read the passage. Take notes on the main points of the reading passage.

The Polynesian Migration

One of the greatest migrations in history, one that perhaps is not traditionally given adequate credit, is the Polynesian migration throughout a 20,000-square-mile area of the Pacific Ocean. Around 4,000 years ago, the Polynesians began spreading out to cover the islands that are in a triangle from Hawaii in the north, to New Zealand in the South, and to Easter Island in the east. The Polynesians managed to cover this vast area of the Pacific Ocean using outrigger canoes, which are a type of vessel composed of two tree trunks joined together by a platform on which humans and animals rode across vast areas of the ocean.

TOPIC OF READING PASSAGE:

main points about the topic:

-

-

Speaking Skill 10: NOTE THE MAIN POINTS AS YOU LISTEN

In the second reading, listening, and speaking integrated task in the Speaking section of the TOEFL iBT, you will also be asked to listen to an academic passage as part of the task. In this part of the integrated task, it is important for you to be able to listen to an academic passage of 1–2 minutes and take notes on the main points of the listening passage as you listen. Look at the following example of a listening passage that is part of the integrated speaking task on the author Isaac Asimov.

Listening Passage

(professor): *Now I'm sure you're all wondering how Asimov managed to write so much. Well, the simple answer is that he did almost nothing except write because that's what he was driven to do.*

Asimov's normal routine was to spend time, a lot of time, writing every day. He usually got up at six o'clock in the morning; he was at work writing by seven-thirty in the morning, and he wrote until ten o'clock in the evening. That's a lot of time to spend writing. This desire to spend so much time writing prompted Asimov himself to say, "Writing is my only interest. Even speaking is an interruption."

As you listen to the passage, you should take notes on the topic and main points of the listening passage. Look at these notes on the topic and main points of the listening passage.

> TOPIC OF LISTENING PASSAGE: how Asimov wrote so much
>
> <u>main points about the topic:</u>
> • Asimov wrote from 7:30 in the morning to 10:00 in the evening
> • Asimov said, "Writing is my only interest"

These notes show that the topic of the listening passage is how Asimov managed to write so much; what Asimov did was to write *from 7:30 in the morning until 10:00 in the evening* daily and to say *"writing is my only interest."*

The following chart outlines the key information you should remember about dealing with the listening passage in the integrated speaking task.

NOTING THE MAIN POINTS IN THE LISTENING PASSAGE	
TOPIC	Make sure that you understand (and take notes on) the *topic* of the listening passage.
MAIN POINTS	Then focus on (and take notes on) the *main points* that are used to support the topic of the listening passage.

SPEAKING EXERCISE 10: Listen to each of the following passages, and note the *topic* and the *main points* that are used to support the topic.

1. Listen to the passage. Take notes on the main points of the listening passage. 🎧

TOPIC OF LISTENING PASSAGE:

<u>main points about the topic:</u>

•

•

2. Listen to the passage. Take notes on the main points of the listening passage. 🎧

TOPIC OF LISTENING PASSAGE:

main points about the topic:

-

-

3. Listen to the passage. Take notes on the main points of the listening passage. 🎧

TOPIC OF LISTENING PASSAGE:

main points about the topic:

-

-

Speaking Skill 11: PLAN BEFORE YOU SPEAK

After you have noted the main points of the reading passage and the main points of the listening passage in the academic integrated reading, listening, and speaking task, you need to read the question and plan your response.

The question will most likely be about how the main points of the reading passage and the main points of the listening passage are related. Look at the following example of a question in the integrated speaking task on the author Isaac Asimov.

Question

How does the information in the professor's lecture add to the information in the reading passage about Isaac Asimov?

You can see that, although the question does not specifically mention "main points" of the reading passage and listening passage, the question is in reality asking you to show how the main points of these two passages are related.

To prepare a plan for your response, you should look at the notes you have taken on the reading passage and the notes you have taken on the listening passage and focus on how the ideas in the two passages are related. Look at the plan for a response to the integrated speaking task on author Isaac Asimov.

Reading Passage = *an author who wrote an amazing amount*

TOPIC OF READING PASSAGE: author Isaac Asimov

main points about Asimov:
- wrote a huge amount of material (more than 500 books)
- wrote on a wide variety of topics (literary analysis, history, physics, chemistry, astronomy, science fiction)

Listening Passage = *how the author accomplished this*

TOPIC OF LISTENING PASSAGE: how Asimov wrote so much

main points about the topic:
- Asimov wrote from 7:30 in the morning to 10:00 in the evening
- Asimov said, "Writing is my only interest"

From this plan, you can see the way that the ideas in the reading passage and the listening passage are related. The plan shows that the reading passage describes *an author who wrote an amazing amount* and the listening passage explains *how the author accomplished this*.

The following chart outlines the key information you should remember about planning before you speak in an integrated speaking task.

PLANNING BEFORE YOU SPEAK	
QUESTION	Study the *question* to determine what is being asked. Expect that the question is asking how the ideas in the reading passage and the listening passage are related.
RELATIONSHIP	Look at the notes you have taken on the reading passage and the listening passage, and focus on the main points or topics of each passage. Then describe how the ideas in each of the two passages are *related*.

SPEAKING EXERCISE 11: Look at the notes that you prepared for the reading passages in Speaking Exercise 9 and the listening passages in Speaking Exercise 10. Read the question for each task. Then prepare a plan for your response. Be sure to note the relationship between the reading passage and the listening passage in your plan.

1. How does the information in the listening passage supplement the information in the reading passage?

2. How is the information in the listening passage related to the information in the reading passage?

3. What interesting point is provided in the listening passage to add to the information in the reading passage?

Speaking Skill 12: MAKE THE RESPONSE

After you have planned your response, you need to make your response. As you make your response, you should think about the following three things: (1) you should start with a topic statement, (2) you should support the topic statement, and (3) you should use transitions to show how the ideas are related.

Look at the plan for a response to the integrated speaking task on author Isaac Asimov and a sample response based on these notes.

Reading Passage = *an author who wrote an amazing amount*

TOPIC OF READING PASSAGE: author Isaac Asimov

main points about Asimov:
• wrote a huge amount of material (more than 500 books)
• wrote on a wide variety of topics (literary analysis,
   history, physics, chemistry, astronomy, science fiction)

Listening Passage = *how the author accomplished this*

TOPIC OF LISTENING PASSAGE: how Asimov wrote so much

main points about the topic:
• Asimov wrote from 7:30 in the morning to 10:00 in the evening
• Asimov said, "Writing is my only interest"

   In this set of materials, the reading passage discusses an author who wrote an amazing amount of material, and the listening passage explains how the author accomplished this.
   The reading passage explains that Asimov wrote a huge amount of material, more than 500 books in total. (In addition), he wrote books on a wide variety of topics (such as) literary analysis, history, physics, chemistry, astronomy, and science fiction.
   The listening passage explains how Asimov managed to accomplish all this work. Asimov wrote all day long, from 7:30 in the morning until 10:00 in the evening. (Moreover), he was interested only in writing, saying, "Writing is my only interest."

You should notice that this response begins with a topic statement showing the relationship between the information in the reading passage and the listening passage. Two supporting paragraphs describing the main points of the reading passage and the listening passage follow the topic statement. The transitions *in addition, such as,* and *moreover* are used to show how the ideas in the supporting paragraphs are related.

The following chart outlines the key information you should remember about making the response.

MAKING THE RESPONSE	
TOPIC	Start your response with a *topic statement* that shows how the ideas in the reading passage and the ideas in the listening passage are related.
SUPPORT	Include the *key points* of the reading passage and the listening passage in your response.
TRANSITIONS	Use *transitions* to show how the ideas are related.

SPEAKING EXERCISE 12: Create responses for the integrated reading, listening, and speaking tasks that you have been working on in Speaking Skills 9–12.

SPEAKING REVIEW EXERCISE (Skills 9–12):
Read the passage. On a piece of paper, take notes on the main points of the reading passage.

The Equity Theory

The equity theory of employee satisfaction in business focuses on comparisons between employees; the basis of this theory is that workers in an organization evaluate their treatment by the organization by comparing their treatment to the treatment of other workers in the organization. According to this theory, workers evaluate their *return for contribution,* what they contribute to the company and what they receive in return for it, and compare their return for contribution to what other employees contribute and receive in return. A worker who receives a return for contribution that is equal to or greater than the return for contribution of other employees will be content, while a worker whose return for contribution is less will not be content.

Listen to the passage. On a piece of paper, take notes on the main points of the listening passage.

Now answer the following question:

How does the information in the listening passage add to the information in the reading passage?

INTEGRATED TASKS (Listening)

There are two integrated tasks that integrate speaking with listening. These two integrated speaking tasks are on a campus topic and on an academic topic.

Speaking Skill 13: NOTE THE MAIN POINTS AS YOU LISTEN

In one of the listening and speaking integrated tasks in the Speaking section of the TOEFL iBT, you will be asked to listen to a passage from a campus setting as part of the task. In this part of the integrated task, it is important for you to be able to listen to a campus passage of 2–3 minutes and take notes on the main points of the listening passage as you listen. Look at the following example of a listening passage that is part of the integrated speaking task.

Listening Passage

(woman)   Hi, Brett.

(man)   Hi, Karen.

(woman)   You don't look too happy, Brett. Is anything the matter?

(man)   You can tell I'm upset just by looking at me?

(woman)   Yeah, it's pretty obvious. You want to tell me what's bothering you?

(man)   Well, it's that I'm having trouble in my economics class, and I just talked to the professor. She didn't seem too sympathetic.

(woman)   She didn't? What's the problem?

(man)   Well, it's that I'm on the baseball team.

(woman)   I know. I've seen you play. But what does that have to do with your economics class?

(man)   It's the away games. That's the problem. The away games are all on the weekend, but usually when we're traveling to another school for a weekend game, we leave on Friday. The team bus usually leaves about noon on Friday.

(woman)   And that has something to do with your economics class?

(man)   Yeah, my economics class meets on Mondays, Wednesdays, and Fridays, in the afternoon.

(woman)   I see. So you miss your economics class once in a while on Friday afternoons?

(man)   Not just once in a while. It's been every Friday for the last four weeks.

(woman)   And you talked to your economics professor about this?

(man)   Yes, I did. And I told her <u>why</u> I missed class on Fridays.

(woman)   But she wasn't very sympathetic you said.

(man)   She wasn't sympathetic at all.

(woman)   I think that's because you've missed so many classes. . . . Listen, have you thought about switching to a different section of the class? I think there's another section of the same class on Tuesdays and Thursdays.

(man)   I hadn't thought about that. Maybe that would be something to consider, since my professor's not at all happy that I miss class so much.

As you listen to the passage, you should take notes on the topic and main points of the listening passage. Look at these notes on the topic and main points of the listening passage.

> TOPIC OF LISTENING PASSAGE: the man's problem and the woman's reaction to it
>
> main points about the problem:
> - man is missing economics class on Fridays because he is on baseball team
> - woman suggests changing to a different section of economics class that does not meet on Fridays

These notes show that the topic of the listening passage is a *problem* the man is having *and the woman's reaction to it,* and the main points about this topic are that the *man is missing his economics class on Fridays because he is on the baseball team,* and the *woman suggests that he change to a different section of the economics class, one that does not meet on Fridays.*

The following chart outlines the key information you should remember about dealing with the listening passage in the integrated speaking task.

NOTING THE MAIN POINTS IN THE LISTENING PASSAGE	
TOPIC	Make sure that you understand (and take notes on) the *topic* of the listening passage.
MAIN POINTS	Then focus on (and take notes on) the *main points* that are used to support the topic of the listening passage.

SPEAKING EXERCISE 13: Listen to each of the following passages, and note the *topic* and the *main points* that are used to support the topic.

1. Listen to the passage. Take notes on the main points of the listening passage. 🎧

TOPIC OF LISTENING PASSAGE:

main points about the topic:

-

-

2. Listen to the passage. Take notes on the main points of the listening passage. 🎧

TOPIC OF LISTENING PASSAGE:

main points about the topic:

-

-

3. Listen to the passage. Take notes on the main points of the listening passage.

TOPIC OF LISTENING PASSAGE:

main points about the topic:

-

-

Speaking Skill 14: PLAN BEFORE YOU SPEAK

After you have noted the main points of the listening passage in the campus integrated listening and speaking task, you need to read the question and plan your response.

The question will most likely be about the main points of the listening passage. Look at the following example of a question in the integrated speaking task on the problem the man is having in his economics class.

Question
How does the woman react to the man's problem?

You can see that, although the question does not specifically mention "main points" of the listening passage, the question is in reality asking you what the main points of the passage are.

To prepare a plan for your response, you should look at the notes you have taken on the listening passage and focus on the main points of the passage. Look at the plan for a response on the integrated speaking task on the problem the man is having in his economics class.

Listening Passage = *a woman's reaction to a man's problem*
TOPIC OF LISTENING PASSAGE: *the man's problem and the woman's reaction to it*
main points about the problem: • *man is missing economics class on Fridays because he is on baseball team*   • *woman suggests changing to a different section of economics class that does not meet on Fridays*

From this plan, you can see that the listening passage is about *a woman's reaction to a man's problem.*

The following chart outlines the key information you should remember about planning before you speak in an integrated speaking task.

PLANNING BEFORE YOU SPEAK	
QUESTION	Study the *question* to determine what is being asked. Expect that the question is asking about the main ideas of the listening passage.
FOCUS	Look at the notes you have taken on the listening passage, and focus on the *main points* of the passage. Then describe the main points of the listening passage.

SPEAKING EXERCISE 14: Look at the notes that you prepared for the listening passages in Speaking Exercise 13. Read the question for each task. Then prepare a plan for your response. Be sure to note the main points of the listening passage.

1. How does the woman seem to feel about the information she gets from the man?

2. How does the woman suggest that the man change his study habits?

3. How does the man respond to the woman's question about an independent study project?

Speaking Skill 15: MAKE THE RESPONSE

After you have planned your response, you need to make your response. As you make your response, you should think about the following three things: (1) you should start with a topic statement, (2) you should support the topic statement, and (3) you should use transitions to show how the ideas are related.

Look at the plan for a response to the independent speaking task on the problem the man is having in his economics class and a sample response based on these notes.

Listening Passage = *a woman's reaction to a man's problem*

TOPIC OF LISTENING PASSAGE: the man's problem and the woman's reaction to it

main points about the problem:
- man is missing economics class on Fridays because he is on baseball team
- woman suggests changing to a different section of economics class that does not meet on Fridays

---

    In this listening passage, two students discuss a problem the man is having and the woman's reaction to it. (First), the man explains that he has the problem that he is missing his economics class on Fridays because he is on the baseball team and he travels to away games on Fridays. (Then), after the woman understands this problem, she suggests that he change to a different section of economics class, one that does not meet on Fridays.

You should notice that this response includes a topic statement followed by several supporting details. The transitions *first* and *then* are used to show how the ideas are related.

The following chart outlines the key information you should remember about making the response.

MAKING THE RESPONSE	
TOPIC	Start your response with a *topic statement* that states the main point of the response.
SUPPORT	Include *details* to support the topic statement.
TRANSITIONS	Use *transitions* to show how the ideas in the response are related.

SPEAKING EXERCISE 15: Create responses for the independent speaking tasks that you have been working on in Speaking Skills 13–15.

SPEAKING REVIEW EXERCISE (Skills 13–15):
Listen to the passage. On a piece of paper, take notes on the main points of the listening passage. 🎧

Now answer the following question:

What does the woman suggest the man can do to deal with his problem?

Speaking Skill 16: NOTE THE MAIN POINTS AS YOU LISTEN

In the second listening and speaking integrated task in the Speaking section of the TOEFL iBT, you will be asked to listen to an academic passage as part of the task. In this part of the integrated task, it is important for you to be able to listen to an academic passage of 2–3 minutes and take notes on the main points of the listening passage as you listen. Look at the following example of a listening passage that is part of an integrated speaking task.

Listening Passage

(professor)   *Today, I'm going to talk about certain types of political characters. One of these types of political characters is called a Hamlet, you know, after the character in the Shakespeare play.*

In Shakespeare's play, Hamlet was a tragic figure, one who spent a lot of time anguishing over what to do in a particularly terrible situation; Hamlet learned that his uncle had murdered Hamlet's father. Hamlet considered what to do in this situation and then he considered still more. He anguished over the decision, he vacillated back and forth, and he anguished some more over the decision.

In political terms, a Hamlet is someone who goes through this sort of decision-making process. A Hamlet is someone who, when faced with a decision, tends to overthink problems, to vacillate, to find it difficult to come to a decision.

As you listen to the passage, you should take notes on the topic and main points of the listening passage. Look at these notes on the topic and main points of the listening passage.

TOPIC OF LISTENING PASSAGE: a type of political character known as a Hamlet

details about a Hamlet:
- Hamlet in Shakespeare's play faced a difficult decision and had a hard time coming to a decision
- a political Hamlet is someone who has a hard time coming to a difficult decision

---

These notes show that the topic of the listening passage is *a type of political character known as a Hamlet,* and the details about a Hamlet are that the character named *Hamlet in Shakespeare's play faced a difficult decision and had a hard time coming to a decision,* and that *a political Hamlet is someone who* also *has a hard time coming to a difficult decision.*

The following chart outlines the key information you should remember about dealing with the listening passage in the integrated speaking task.

NOTING THE MAIN POINTS IN THE LISTENING PASSAGE	
TOPIC	Make sure that you understand (and take notes on) the *topic* of the listening passage.
MAIN POINTS	Then focus on (and take notes on) the *main points* that are used to support the topic of the listening passage.

SPEAKING EXERCISE 16: Listen to each of the following passages, and note the *topic* and the *main points* that are used to support the topic.

1. Listen to the passage. Take notes on the main points of the listening passage. 🎧

TOPIC OF LISTENING PASSAGE:

main points about the topic:

•

•

2. Listen to the passage. Take notes on the main points of the listening passage. 🎧

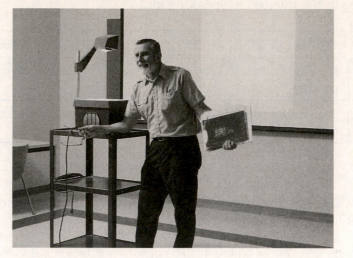

TOPIC OF LISTENING PASSAGE:

main points about the topic:

-

-

3. Listen to the passage. Take notes on the main points of the listening passage. 🎧

TOPIC OF LISTENING PASSAGE:

main points about the topic:

-

-

Speaking Skill 17: PLAN BEFORE YOU SPEAK

After you have noted the main points of the listening passage in the academic integrated listening and speaking task, you need to read the question and plan your response.

The question will most likely be about the main points of the listening passage. Look at the following example of a question in the integrated speaking task on a political character called a Hamlet.

Question

How is a certain type of political character described in the lecture?

You can see that, although the question does not specifically mention "main points" of the listening passage, the question is in reality asking you what the main points of the passage are.

To prepare a plan for your response, you should look at the notes you have taken on the listening passage and focus on the main points of the passage. Look at the plan for a response on the integrated speaking task on a certain type of political character.

Listening Passage = *a description of a political character*

TOPIC OF LISTENING PASSAGE: *a type of political character known as a Hamlet*

details about a Hamlet:
- *Hamlet in Shakespeare's play faced a difficult decision and had a hard time coming to a decision*
- *a political Hamlet is someone who has a hard time coming to a difficult decision*

From this plan, you can see that the listening passage is about a *description of a political character.*

The following chart outlines the key information you should remember about planning before you speak in an integrated speaking task.

PLANNING BEFORE YOU SPEAK	
QUESTION	Study the *question* to determine what is being asked. Expect that the question is asking about the main ideas of the listening passage.
FOCUS	Look at the notes you have taken on the listening passage, and focus on the *main points* of the passage. Then describe the main points of the listening passage.

SPEAKING EXERCISE 17: Look at the notes that you prepared for the listening passages in Speaking Exercise 16. Read the question for each task. Then prepare a plan for your response. Be sure to note the main points of the listening passage.

1. What can one learn from the listening passage about the Bank Holiday of 1933?

2. What can be learned from the listening passage about a definition of creativity?

3. According to the listening passage, how did the Amazon get its name?

Speaking Skill 18: MAKE THE RESPONSE

After you have planned your response, you need to make your response. As you make your response, you should think about the following three things: (1) you should start with a topic statement, (2) you should support the topic statement, and (3) you should use transitions to show how the ideas are related.

Look at the plan for a response to the independent speaking task on a certain political character and a sample response based on these notes.

Listening Passage = *a description of a political character*

TOPIC OF LISTENING PASSAGE: *a type of political character known as a Hamlet*

details about a Hamlet:
- *Hamlet in Shakespeare's play faced a difficult decision and had a hard time coming to a decision*
- *a political Hamlet is someone who has a hard time coming to a difficult decision*

   In this listening passage, the professor discusses a certain type of political character that is known as a Hamlet. Hamlet was a character in a play by Shakespeare, and in the play Hamlet faced a difficult decision and had a hard time coming to a decision. A political person who has a hard time coming to a difficult decision can (therefore) *be called a Hamlet.*

You should notice that this response includes a topic statement followed by several supporting details. The transition *therefore* is used to show how the ideas are related.

The following chart outlines the key information you should remember about making the response.

MAKING THE RESPONSE	
TOPIC	Start your response with a *topic statement* that states the main point of the response.
SUPPORT	Include *details* to support the topic statement.
TRANSITIONS	Use *transitions* to show how the ideas in the response are related.

SPEAKING EXERCISE 18: Create responses for the independent speaking tasks that you have been working on in Speaking Skills 16–18.

SPEAKING REVIEW EXERCISE (Skills 16–18):
Listen to the passage. On a piece of paper, take notes on the main points of the listening passage.

Now answer the following question:

What points does the professor make about SAD?

SPEAKING POST-TEST

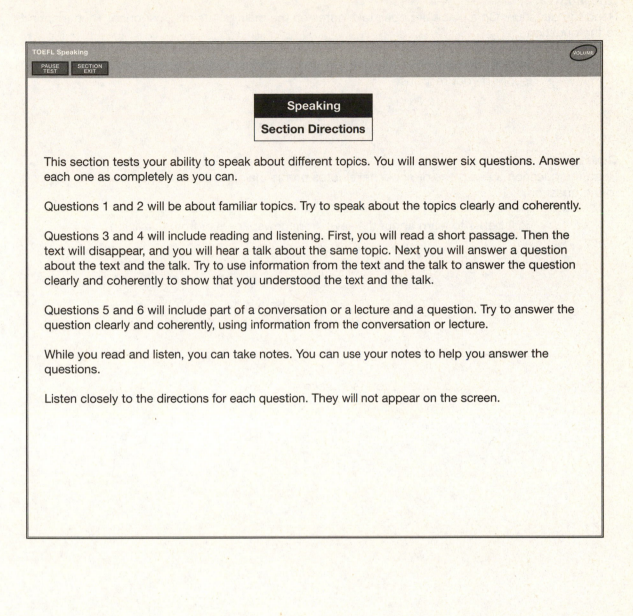

PAUSE TEST   SECTION EXIT

VOLUME

Speaking

Section Directions

This section tests your ability to speak about different topics. You will answer six questions. Answer each one as completely as you can.

Questions 1 and 2 will be about familiar topics. Try to speak about the topics clearly and coherently.

Questions 3 and 4 will include reading and listening. First, you will read a short passage. Then the text will disappear, and you will hear a talk about the same topic. Next you will answer a question about the text and the talk. Try to use information from the text and the talk to answer the question clearly and coherently to show that you understood the text and the talk.

Questions 5 and 6 will include part of a conversation or a lecture and a question. Try to answer the question clearly and coherently, using information from the conversation or lecture.

While you read and listen, you can take notes. You can use your notes to help you answer the questions.

Listen closely to the directions for each question. They will not appear on the screen.

Question 1

Read the question. On a piece of paper, take notes on the main points of a response. Then respond to the question.

Which person who is living today do you admire most? Use reasons to support your response.

Question 2

Read the question. On a piece of paper, take notes on the main points of a response. Then respond to the question.

Is it better to learn about the news from newspapers or from television?

① she is a
I admire most my mother x strong person & ② responsible women
she is a teacher, she is working
she takes care of us, she helped us c̄
study, she gives us all factors for success
eventhough she was alone after death
of my brother, she continued to do
her best with us, & she never gave up

get
① I can watch at it & international news from Television.
② I can watch live news
③ convient. lying, or eating my lunch.
I can learn dot & intr news from

Question 3
Read the passage. On a piece of paper, take notes on the main points of the reading passage.

Notice from University Food Services

University Food Services is sorry to notify any students holding meal cards that the main cafeteria will be closed until November 1. It has been necessary to close the main cafeteria for the week of October 24 to November 1 in order to make much-needed repairs. During the period that the main cafeteria is closed, any students who have meal cards may use their meal cards at the three snack bars on campus. We recognize that this arrangement will be inconvenient both for students holding meal cards and for students who regularly purchase meals at the three snack bars. Please accept our sincere apologies for this inconvenience.

Listen to the passage. On a piece of paper, take notes on the main points of the listening passage. 🎧

Now answer the following question:

How does the information in the listening passage add to the information included in the reading passage?

from the 3 snacks bar.
main cafe closed.
fine

Question 4

Read the passage. On a piece of paper, take notes on the main points of the reading passage.

Social Environments

It is important for an effective teacher to recognize that various types of social environments can be established in the classroom based upon the goals that are to be met. Three of the major types of social environments that an effective teacher can work to establish are a cooperative environment, a competitive environment, and an individualistic environment. In a cooperative social environment in the classroom, the students work together to complete tasks. In a competitive social environment, students try to come up with better answers more quickly or efficiently than other students. In an individualistic social environment, students work by themselves to come up with the best answers that they can working alone.

Listen to the passage. On a piece of paper, take notes on the main points of the listening passage. 🎧

Now answer the following question:

How does the information in the listening passage supplement the information in the reading passage?

steps to ensure social enviv
is good for some task

① cross students

② cross students

② cross the students.

Question 5
Listen to the passage. On a piece of paper, take notes on the main points of the listening passage. 🎧

Now answer the following question:

How does the man feel about the problem the woman has?

Question 6
Listen to the passage. On a piece of paper, take notes on the main points of the listening passage. 🎧

Now answer the following question:

What points does the professor make about the planet Mars?

Turn to pages 94–105 to *assess* the skills used in the test,
score the test using the Speaking Scoring Criteria, and *record* your results.

SPEAKING MINI-TEST 1

PAUSE TEST   SECTION EXIT   VOLUME

Speaking

Section Directions

This section tests your ability to speak about different topics. You will answer three questions. Answer each one as completely as you can.

Question 1 will be about a familiar topic. Try to speak about the topic clearly and coherently.

Question 2 will include reading and listening. First, you will read a short passage about a topic. Then the text will disappear, and you will hear a talk about the same topic. Next you will answer a question about the passage and the talk. Try to answer the question clearly and coherently to show that you understood the passage and the talk.

Question 3 will include part of a conversation or a lecture and a question. Try to answer the question clearly and coherently, using information from the conversation or lecture.

While you read and listen, you can take notes. You can use your notes to help you answer the questions.

Listen closely to the directions for each question. They will not appear on the screen.

Questions 1–3

Question 1

Read the question. On a piece of paper, take notes on the main points of a response. Then respond to the question.

> If you were the leader of your country, what would you do? Use reasons and details to support your response.
>
> | Preparation Time: 15 seconds |
> | Response Time: 45 seconds |

Question 2

Read the passage. On a piece of paper, take notes on the main points of the reading passage.

> | Reading Time: 45 seconds |

Part of the syllabus in a history class

One of the requirements for this class is that you watch a number of films on historical topics. You will be given a list of twenty films, and you are required to watch at least twelve of the twenty films. After you watch each film, you are to write a report summarizing the key information in the film. (If you want, you may turn in reports on more than twelve films for extra credit.) All twenty films are on reserve in the library, and you may watch them in one of the viewing rooms on the second floor of the library.

Listen to the passage. On a piece of paper, take notes on the main points of the listening passage. 🎧

Now answer the following question:

> How do the students seem to feel about the history class assignment?
>
> | Preparation Time: 30 seconds |
> | Response Time: 60 seconds |

Question 3

Listen to the passage. On a piece of paper, take notes on the main points of the listening passage. 🎧

Now answer the following question:

How are glaciers formed?

Preparation Time: 20 seconds
Response Time: 60 seconds

Turn to pages 94–105 to *assess* the skills used in the test,
score the test using the Speaking Scoring Criteria, and *record* your results.

Glaciers — how they are formed.
mass of ice that is moving   pressure under snow for
forms where snow sufficiently accumulate. then melt → underneath.
accumulated →snow → ice crystals pack ice large crystals
sufficient ice.   Flakes

then pack ice move. and glacer formed.

① snow accumul
② pressure + snow
③ small ice crystals come together — packed — large crystals.
④ large crystals move.
   packed.

SPEAKING MINI-TEST 2

PAUSE TEST | SECTION EXIT

VOLUME

Speaking
Section Directions

This section tests your ability to speak about different topics. You will answer three questions. Answer each one as completely as you can.

Question 1 will be about a familiar topic. Try to speak about the topic clearly and coherently.

Question 2 will include reading and listening. First, you will read a short passage about a topic. Then the text will disappear, and you will hear a talk about the same topic. Next you will answer a question about the passage and the talk. Try to answer the question clearly and coherently to show that you understood the passage and the talk.

Question 3 will include part of a conversation or a lecture and a question. Try to answer the question clearly and coherently, using information from the conversation or lecture.

While you read and listen, you can take notes. You can use your notes to help you answer the questions.

Listen closely to the directions for each question. They will not appear on the screen.

Questions 1–3

Question 1

Read the question. On a piece of paper, take notes on the main points of a response. Then respond to the question.

> Do you think it is better to get up early in the morning or sleep in until later? Use reasons and details to support your response.

> | Preparation Time: 15 seconds |
> | Response Time: 45 seconds |

Question 2

Read the passage. On a piece of paper, take notes on the main points of the reading passage.

> | Reading Time: 45 seconds |

Leadership Roles

Have you ever considered the various roles that a group leader might take on? There can be many different kinds of leadership roles in groups; two of the many possible kinds of leadership roles are *instrumental* leadership and *expressive* leadership. Instrumental leadership is group leadership that emphasizes the completion of tasks by the group. Instrumental leadership is focused on getting the task done. Expressive leadership is different from instrumental leadership. Expressive leadership is leadership that is concerned with the well-being of the group; expressive leadership is leadership that is concerned with ensuring that all members of the group are comfortable working together.

Listen to the passage. On a piece of paper, take notes on the main points of the listening passage. 🎧

Now answer the following question:

> How does the information in the listening passage add to the information in the reading passage?

> | Preparation Time: 30 seconds |
> | Response Time: 60 seconds |

Question 3

Listen to the passage. On a piece of paper, take notes on the main points of the listening passage. 🎧

Now answer the following question:

How do the students seem to feel about what will be discussed at the student council meeting?

| Preparation Time: 20 seconds |
| Response Time: 60 seconds |

Turn to pages 94–105 to *assess* the skills used in the test,
score the test using the Speaking Scoring Criteria, and *record* your results.

*both reading
& listening is about
ROLES of leadership groups*

*on the reading
we learned that —*

*• student cancell.
meeting open meting
↳ discussion about
final exam schedule
to change final exam*

*schedule want to reschedule 3 day
they want to
schedule to
try to fix
exam as it now*

*instead of 6
the final*

SPEAKING MINI-TEST 3

PAUSE TEST   SECTION EXIT   VOLUME

Speaking

Section Directions

This section tests your ability to speak about different topics. You will answer three questions. Answer each one as completely as you can.

Question 1 will be about a familiar topic. Try to speak about the topic clearly and coherently.

Question 2 will include reading and listening. First, you will read a short passage about a topic. Then the text will disappear, and you will hear a talk about the same topic. Next you will answer a question about the passage and the talk. Try to answer the question clearly and coherently to show that you understood the passage and the talk.

Question 3 will include part of a conversation or a lecture and a question. Try to answer the question clearly and coherently, using information from the conversation or lecture.

While you read and listen, you can take notes. You can use your notes to help you answer the questions.

Listen closely to the directions for each question. They will not appear on the screen.

Questions 1–3

Question 1

Read the question. On a piece of paper, take notes on the main points of a response. Then respond to the question.

Which place in your hometown would you like to take visitors to see?

> Preparation Time: 15 seconds
> Response Time: 45 seconds

Question 2

Read the passage. On a piece of paper, take notes on the main points of the reading passage.

> Reading Time: 45 seconds

Notice posted around the library

The library is a place for reading, working on research, or studying only. It is not a concert hall. It is not a chat room. It is not a dining room. It is not a motel. This means that you may not play loud music in the library, you may not talk in a loud voice in the library, you may not have food or drink in the library, and you may not stretch out and go to sleep in the library. Anyone who does not follow these rules to the letter will be asked to leave the library immediately.

Listen to the passage. On a piece of paper, take notes on the main points of the listening passage. 🎧

Now answer the following question:

How do the students react to the notice posted in the library?

> Preparation Time: 30 seconds
> Response Time: 60 seconds

Question 3

Listen to the passage. On a piece of paper, take notes on the main points of the listening passage.

Now answer the following question:

Why does the professor use the example of split infinitives?

| Preparation Time: 20 seconds |
| Response Time: 60 seconds |

Turn to pages 94–105 to *assess* the skills used in the test,
score the test using the Speaking Scoring Criteria, and *record* your results.

SPEAKING MINI-TEST 4

PAUSE TEST SECTION EXIT

VOLUME

Speaking

Section Directions

This section tests your ability to speak about different topics. You will answer three questions. Answer each one as completely as you can.

Question 1 will be about a familiar topic. Try to speak about the topic clearly and coherently.

Question 2 will include reading and listening. First, you will read a short passage about a topic. Then the text will disappear, and you will hear a talk about the same topic. Next you will answer a question about the passage and the talk. Try to answer the question clearly and coherently to show that you understood the passage and the talk.

Question 3 will include part of a conversation or a lecture and a question. Try to answer the question clearly and coherently, using information from the conversation or lecture.

While you read and listen, you can take notes. You can use your notes to help you answer the questions.

Listen closely to the directions for each question. They will not appear on the screen.

Question 1

Read the question. On a piece of paper, take notes on the main points of a response. Then respond to the question.

> Do you prefer to take essay exams or multiple-choice exams? Use reasons and details to support your response.

> | |
> |---|
> | Preparation Time: 15 seconds |
> | Response Time: 45 seconds |

Question 2

Read the passage. On a piece of paper, take notes on the main points of the reading passage.

> | |
> |---|
> | Reading Time: 45 seconds |

Nullification

The issue of nullification was one that was faced by the United States early in the history of the country. As the country was becoming established, there was a lack of clarification as to the balance of power between the states and the federal government. Nullification was a doctrine by which states believed they could nullify, or refuse to accept, laws passed by the federal government of the United States. In other words, states that believed in their right to nullification believed that they had the authority to reject laws passed by the federal government; the federal government, of course, believed that the states did not have the right to reject federal laws.

Listen to the passage. On a piece of paper, take notes on the main points of the listening passage.

Now answer the following question:

> How does the information in the listening passage add to what is explained in the reading passage?

> | |
> |---|
> | Preparation Time: 30 seconds |
> | Response Time: 60 seconds |

Question 3

Listen to the passage. On a piece of paper, take notes on the main points of the listening passage. 🎧

Now answer the following question:

What is happening with the students' assignments for their psychology class?

> Preparation Time: 20 seconds
> Response Time: 60 seconds

Turn to pages 94–105 to *assess* the skills used in the test,
score the test using the Speaking Scoring Criteria, and *record* your results.

SPEAKING MINI-TEST 5

PAUSE TEST | SECTION EXIT

VOLUME

Speaking

Section Directions

This section tests your ability to speak about different topics. You will answer three questions. Answer each one as completely as you can.

Question 1 will be about a familiar topic. Try to speak about the topic clearly and coherently.

Question 2 will include reading and listening. First, you will read a short passage about a topic. Then the text will disappear, and you will hear a talk about the same topic. Next you will answer a question about the passage and the talk. Try to answer the question clearly and coherently to show that you understood the passage and the talk.

Question 3 will include part of a conversation or a lecture and a question. Try to answer the question clearly and coherently, using information from the conversation or lecture.

While you read and listen, you can take notes. You can use your notes to help you answer the questions.

Listen closely to the directions for each question. They will not appear on the screen.

Questions 1–3

Question 1

Read the question. On a piece of paper, take notes on the main points of a response. Then respond to the question.

> What are the most important characteristics of a good friend? Use examples to support your response.

> Preparation Time: 15 seconds
> Response Time: 45 seconds

Question 2

Read the passage. On a piece of paper, take notes on the main points of the reading passage.

> Reading Time: 45 seconds

A notice in the Administration Building

Eight positions for student assistants are available in the Administration Building for the coming academic year. These positions are open to full-time students who have completed at least 60 units with a minimum grade-point average of 3.0. Students applying for these positions must be available to work either from 9:00 AM to noon or from 1:00 to 4:00 PM Monday through Friday. They must also have basic computer and telephone skills. Applications may be obtained as of now at the reception desk in the Administration Building; they must be completed and submitted no later than 4:00 PM this coming Friday.

Listen to the passage. On a piece of paper, take notes on the main points of the listening passage.

Now answer the following question:

> How do the students respond to the notice about the positions in the Administration Building?

> Preparation Time: 30 seconds
> Response Time: 60 seconds

Question 3

Listen to the passage. On a piece of paper, take notes on the main points of the listening passage. 🎧

Now answer the following question:

How is the concept of zero-sum games related to the study of economic systems?

> Preparation Time: 20 seconds
> Response Time: 60 seconds

Turn to pages 94–105 to *assess* the skills used in the test,
score the test using the Speaking Scoring Criteria, and *record* your results.

SPEAKING MINI-TEST 6

PAUSE TEST   SECTION EXIT   VOLUME

Speaking

Section Directions

This section tests your ability to speak about different topics. You will answer three questions. Answer each one as completely as you can.

Question 1 will be about a familiar topic. Try to speak about the topic clearly and coherently.

Question 2 will include reading and listening. First, you will read a short passage about a topic. Then the text will disappear, and you will hear a talk about the same topic. Next you will answer a question about the passage and the talk. Try to answer the question clearly and coherently to show that you understood the passage and the talk.

Question 3 will include part of a conversation or a lecture and a question. Try to answer the question clearly and coherently, using information from the conversation or lecture.

While you read and listen, you can take notes. You can use your notes to help you answer the questions.

Listen closely to the directions for each question. They will not appear on the screen.

Questions 1–3

Question 1

Read the question. On a piece of paper, take notes on the main points of a response. Then respond to the question.

> If you won a million dollars, would you save most of it or spend most of it? Use reasons and details to support your response.

> Preparation Time: 15 seconds
> Response Time: 45 seconds

Question 2

Read the passage. On a piece of paper, take notes on the main points of the reading passage.

> Reading Time: 45 seconds

Formation of the Solar System

Around 5 billion years ago, what is today our Solar System was most likely a spinning cloud of gas and dust. The vast majority of gas and dust in this cloud began clumping together to form our Sun, and some of the rest of the material began forming clumps that became the planets in our Solar System, including our Earth. As our planet came together, it formed into a globe with a layered structure. The way that this layered structure ended up was with the heavier material in the middle of the globe and the lighter material on the outside surrounding the heavier material.

Listen to the passage. On a piece of paper, take notes on the main points of the listening passage. 🎧

Now answer the following question:

> How does the information in the listening passage add to what is explained in the reading passage?

> Preparation Time: 30 seconds
> Response Time: 60 seconds

Question 3

Listen to the passage. On a piece of paper, take notes on the main points of the listening passage. 🎧

Now answer the following question:

How are the students dealing with the situation surrounding the guest speaker?

Preparation Time: 20 seconds
Response Time: 60 seconds

Turn to pages 94–105 to *assess* the skills used in the test,
score the test using the Speaking Scoring Criteria, and *record* your results.

SPEAKING MINI-TEST 7

PAUSE TEST | SECTION EXIT

VOLUME

Speaking
Section Directions

This section tests your ability to speak about different topics. You will answer three questions. Answer each one as completely as you can.

Question 1 will be about a familiar topic. Try to speak about the topic clearly and coherently.

Question 2 will include reading and listening. First, you will read a short passage about a topic. Then the text will disappear, and you will hear a talk about the same topic. Next you will answer a question about the passage and the talk. Try to answer the question clearly and coherently to show that you understood the passage and the talk.

Question 3 will include part of a conversation or a lecture and a question. Try to answer the question clearly and coherently, using information from the conversation or lecture.

While you read and listen, you can take notes. You can use your notes to help you answer the questions.

Listen closely to the directions for each question. They will not appear on the screen.

Questions 1–3

Question 1

Read the question. On a piece of paper, take notes on the main points of a response. Then respond to the question.

> What do you dislike most about studying English? Use reasons and details to support your response.

> | Preparation Time: 15 seconds |
> | Response Time: 45 seconds |

Question 2

Read the passage. On a piece of paper, take notes on the main points of the reading passage.

> | Reading Time: 45 seconds |

Part of a syllabus in a political science class

Please note that this political science class is a discussion class. This means that you must complete the assigned reading before each class and be prepared to take part in a discussion of the assigned reading. The reading list is attached, and you must complete the assigned reading from the reading list before you come to class. If you have not finished the assigned reading, do not bother to come to class. If you do not plan on taking part in class discussions, do not come to class. If this does not sound good to you, I will be delighted to sign a drop card so that you can transfer to a different class.

Listen to the passage. On a piece of paper, take notes on the main points of the listening passage. 🎧

Now answer the following question:

> How do the students seem to feel about the professor's policy on class discussions?

> | Preparation Time: 30 seconds |
> | Response Time: 60 seconds |

Question 3

Listen to the passage. On a piece of paper, take notes on the main points of the listening passage.

Now answer the following question:

What points does the professor make about a certain kind of response from the public?

> Preparation Time: 20 seconds
> Response Time: 60 seconds

Turn to pages 94–105 to *assess* the skills used in the test,
score the test using the Speaking Scoring Criteria, and *record* your results.

SPEAKING MINI-TEST 8

TOEFL Speaking

PAUSE
TEST

SECTION
EXIT

VOLUME

Speaking

Section Directions

This section tests your ability to speak about different topics. You will answer three questions. Answer each one as completely as you can.

Question 1 will be about a familiar topic. Try to speak about the topic clearly and coherently.

Question 2 will include reading and listening. First, you will read a short passage about a topic. Then the text will disappear, and you will hear a talk about the same topic. Next you will answer a question about the passage and the talk. Try to answer the question clearly and coherently to show that you understood the passage and the talk.

Question 3 will include part of a conversation or a lecture and a question. Try to answer the question clearly and coherently, using information from the conversation or lecture.

While you read and listen, you can take notes. You can use your notes to help you answer the questions.

Listen closely to the directions for each question. They will not appear on the screen.

Questions 1–3

Question 1

Read the question. On a piece of paper, take notes on the main points of a response. Then respond to the question.

> Would you prefer to go to a big party or a small gathering with friends?
> Use specific reasons and details to support your response.

| Preparation Time: 15 seconds |
| Response Time: 45 seconds |

Question 2

Read the passage. On a piece of paper, take notes on the main points of the reading passage.

| Reading Time: 45 seconds |

Somnambulism

Somnambulism, or sleepwalking, is a sleep disorder that can occur in both children and adults. Its causes are not known but are thought to be related to fatigue, severe exhaustion, anxiety, or reaction to drugs. While someone is sleepwalking, he or she may take part in simple actions such as sitting up or getting up and walking around before returning to bed; more complex activities such as getting dressed, washing dishes, moving furniture, and even operating machines such as cars have been noted among some sleepwalkers. Some episodes of sleepwalking are very brief, lasting only seconds or minutes; longer episodes can last an hour or more.

Listen to the passage. On a piece of paper, take notes on the main points of the listening passage.

Now answer the following question:

> How does the information in the listening passage add to what is explained in the reading passage?

| Preparation Time: 30 seconds |
| Response Time: 60 seconds |

Question 3

Listen to the passage. On a piece of paper, take notes on the main points of the listening passage. 🎧

Now answer the following question:

What possible solutions does the woman offer to the man's problem?

| Preparation Time: 20 seconds |
| Response Time: 60 seconds |

Turn to pages 94–105 to *assess* the skills used in the test,
score the test using the Speaking Scoring Criteria, and *record* your results.

SPEAKING COMPLETE TEST 1

TOEFL Speaking

PAUSE
TEST

SECTION
EXIT

VOLUME

Speaking

Section Directions

This section tests your ability to speak about different topics. You will answer six questions. Answer each one as completely as you can.

Questions 1 and 2 will be about familiar topics. Try to speak about the topics clearly and coherently.

Questions 3 and 4 will include reading and listening. First, you will read a short passage. Then the text will disappear, and you will hear a talk about the same topic. Next you will answer a question about the text and the talk. Try to use information from the text and the talk to answer the question clearly and coherently to show that you understood the text and the talk.

Questions 5 and 6 will include part of a conversation or a lecture and a question. Try to answer the question clearly and coherently, using information from the conversation or lecture.

While you read and listen, you can take notes. You can use your notes to help you answer the questions.

Listen closely to the directions for each question. They will not appear on the screen.

Questions 1–6

Question 1

Read the question. On a piece of paper, take notes on the main points of a response. Then respond to the question.

What would be your dream job? Use reasons and details to support your response.

Preparation Time: 15 seconds
Response Time: 45 seconds

Question 2

Read the question. On a piece of paper, take notes on the main points of a response. Then respond to the question.

Would you prefer to write a paper by yourself or with a group? Use reasons and details to support your response.

Preparation Time: 15 seconds
Response Time: 45 seconds

Question 3

Read the passage. On a piece of paper, take notes on the main points of the reading passage.

Reading Time: 45 seconds

Announcement from the Music Department

The Spring Show is an annual program of vocal and instrumental music to celebrate the spring season. Tickets for this fantastic event will go on sale for students at 9:00 A.M. on Monday, March 1, at the music auditorium ticket office. Any tickets that are still available will go on sale to the public on Monday, March 8. Get your tickets early for this fabulous annual event because they always sell out soon after they go on sale to the public. Get your tickets early so that you will not have to miss out on this fabulous event.

Listen to the passage. On a piece of paper, take notes on the main points of the listening passage.

Now answer the following question:

How do the students react to the notice about the Spring Show?

Preparation Time: 30 seconds
Response Time: 60 seconds

Question 4

Read the passage. On a piece of paper, take notes on the main points of the reading passage.

Reading Time: 45 seconds

Great Ape Communication

Quite a few scientific studies have been conducted on communication by the great apes, a group of primates composed of gorillas, chimpanzees, and orangutans. What has been concluded in these studies is that the great apes communicate in a variety of ways that include, but are not limited to, facial expressions, gestures with their appendages, and a variety of calls. The large primates use this wide variety of methods of communication to express a broad range of ideas to other members of their group, such as anger, fear, approaching danger, dominance over the group, or acceptance of members into the group.

Listen to the passage. On a piece of paper, take notes on the main points of the listening passage. 🎧

Now answer the following question:

How does the information in the listening passage add to what is explained in the reading passage?

Preparation Time: 30 seconds
Response Time: 60 seconds

Question 5

Listen to the passage. On a piece of paper, take notes on the main points of the listening passage. 🎧

Now answer the following question:

How is the woman dealing with the problem she is facing?

Preparation Time: 20 seconds
Response Time: 60 seconds

Question 6

Listen to the passage. On a piece of paper, take notes on the main points of the listening passage. 🎧

Now answer the following question:

How does the professor describe mercantilism?

Preparation Time: 20 seconds
Response Time: 60 seconds

Turn to pages 94–105 to *assess* the skills used in the test,
score the test using the Speaking Scoring Criteria, and *record* your results.

SPEAKING COMPLETE TEST 2

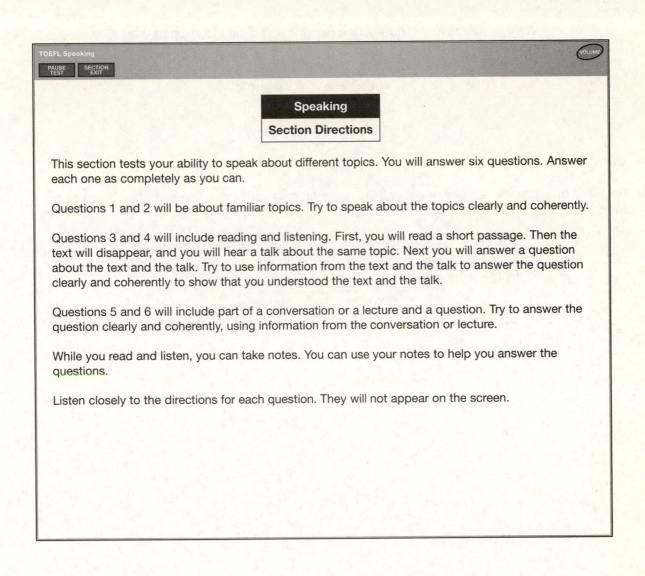

TOEFL Speaking

PAUSE TEST   SECTION EXIT   VOLUME

Speaking
Section Directions

This section tests your ability to speak about different topics. You will answer six questions. Answer each one as completely as you can.

Questions 1 and 2 will be about familiar topics. Try to speak about the topics clearly and coherently.

Questions 3 and 4 will include reading and listening. First, you will read a short passage. Then the text will disappear, and you will hear a talk about the same topic. Next you will answer a question about the text and the talk. Try to use information from the text and the talk to answer the question clearly and coherently to show that you understood the text and the talk.

Questions 5 and 6 will include part of a conversation or a lecture and a question. Try to answer the question clearly and coherently, using information from the conversation or lecture.

While you read and listen, you can take notes. You can use your notes to help you answer the questions.

Listen closely to the directions for each question. They will not appear on the screen.

Question 1

Read the question. On a piece of paper, take notes on the main points of a response. Then respond to the question.

What is your favorite movie? Use reasons and details to support your response.

> Preparation Time: 15 seconds
> Response Time: 45 seconds

Question 2

Read the question. On a piece of paper, take notes on the main points of a response. Then respond to the question.

Do you think it is better to tell the truth and hurt someone's feelings or tell a little lie to keep from hurting the person? Use reasons and details to support your response.

> Preparation Time: 15 seconds
> Response Time: 45 seconds

Question 3

Read the passage. On a piece of paper, take notes on the main points of the reading passage.

Reading Time: 45 seconds

A notice for students in the Business Department

A limited number of internships in local businesses are available for the coming semester. An internship is an unpaid position that requires ten hours of work per week for twelve weeks. Students who are selected for the internship program must sign up for Business 500 and submit reports on their internship to the internship advisor; three graduate units will be awarded for successful completion of Business 500. To apply for an internship, pick up an application from the Business Department office, fill it out, and submit it along with references from three professors in the Business Department by May 1.

Listen to the passage. On a piece of paper, take notes on the main points of the listening passage.

Now answer the following question:

How do the students seem to feel about the internships offered by the Business Department?

Preparation Time: 30 seconds
Response Time: 60 seconds

Question 4

Read the passage. On a piece of paper, take notes on the main points of the reading passage.

> Reading Time: 45 seconds

Supersonic Speed

The terms "subsonic" and "supersonic" are used to describe the speed of various aircraft in relation to the speed of sound. Subsonic aircraft fly at speeds that are slower than the speed of sound, and supersonic aircraft fly at speeds that are faster than the speed of sound. Austrian physicist Ernst Mach (1838–1916) was a pioneer in the study of objects moving faster than the speed of sound and the shock waves that they produce; as a result, the term "Mach" is used to describe the speed of supersonic aircraft. An aircraft flying at Mach 1 is flying at the speed of sound, and an aircraft flying at twice the speed of sound is flying at Mach 2.

Listen to the passage. On a piece of paper, take notes on the main points of the listening passage.

Now answer the following question:

How does the information in the listening passage add to what is explained in the reading passage?

> Preparation Time: 30 seconds
> Response Time: 60 seconds

Question 5

Listen to the passage. On a piece of paper, take notes on the main points of the listening passage. 🎧

Now answer the following question:

How are the students dealing with the project they are working on?

Preparation Time: 20 seconds
Response Time: 60 seconds

Question 6

Listen to the passage. On a piece of paper, take notes on the main points of the listening passage. 🎧

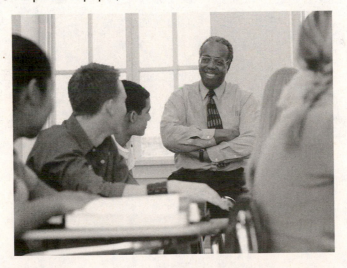

Now answer the following question:

How does the professor describe multiple personality disorder?

Preparation Time: 20 seconds
Response Time: 60 seconds

Turn to pages 94–105 to *assess* the skills used in the test,
score the test using the Speaking Scoring Criteria, and *record* your results.

SPEAKING ASSESSMENT AND SCORING

For the Speaking test sections in this book, it is possible to do the following:

- *assess* the skills used in the Speaking Pre-Test, Speaking Post-Test, Speaking Mini-Tests, and Speaking Complete Tests
- *score* the Speaking Pre-Test, Speaking Post-Test, Speaking Mini-Tests, and Speaking Complete Tests sections using the Speaking Scoring Criteria
- *record* your test results

ASSESSING SPEAKING SKILLS

After you complete each Speaking task on a Speaking Pre-Test, Speaking Post-Test, Speaking Mini-Test, or Speaking Complete Test section, put checkmarks in the appropriate boxes in the following checklists. This will help you assess how well you have used the skills presented in the textbook.

	SKILL-ASSESSMENT CHECKLIST Speaking Independent Tasks, Free Choice: Skills 1–2	SPEAKING DIAGNOSTIC PRE-TEST, Question 1	SPEAKING REVIEW EXERCISE (Skills 1–2)	SPEAKING POST-TEST, Question 1	SPEAKING MINI-TEST 1, Question 1	SPEAKING MINI-TEST 3, Question 1	SPEAKING MINI-TEST 5, Question 1	SPEAKING MINI-TEST 7, Question 1	SPEAKING COMPLETE TEST 1, Question 1	SPEAKING COMPLETE TEST 2, Question 1
SKILL 1	I read the **question** carefully.									
SKILL 1	I included an introduction, supporting ideas, and a conclusion in my **plan**.									
SKILL 2	I began with an **introduction**.									
SKILL 2	I used strong **supporting ideas**.									
SKILL 2	I used **transitions** to connect the supporting ideas.									
SKILL 2	I ended with a **conclusion**.									

	SPEAKING DIAGNOSTIC PRE-TEST, Question 2	SPEAKING REVIEW EXERCISE (Skills 3–4)	SPEAKING POST-TEST, Question 2	SPEAKING MINI-TEST 2, Question 1	SPEAKING MINI-TEST 4, Question 1	SPEAKING MINI-TEST 6, Question 1	SPEAKING MINI-TEST 8, Question 1	SPEAKING COMPLETE TEST 1, Question 2	SPEAKING COMPLETE TEST 2, Question 2
SKILL-ASSESSMENT CHECKLIST **Speaking Independent Tasks, Paired Choice: Skills 3–4**									
SKILL 3 — I read the **question** carefully.									
SKILL 3 — I included an introduction, supporting ideas, and a conclusion in my **plan**.									
SKILL 4 — I began with an **introduction**.									
SKILL 4 — I used strong **supporting ideas**.									
SKILL 4 — I used **transitions** to connect the supporting ideas.									
SKILL 4 — I ended with a **conclusion**.									

		SPEAKING DIAGNOSTIC PRE-TEST, Question 3	SPEAKING REVIEW EXERCISE (Skills 5–8)	SPEAKING POST-TEST, Question 3	SPEAKING MINI-TEST 1, Question 2	SPEAKING MINI-TEST 3, Question 2	SPEAKING MINI-TEST 5, Question 2	SPEAKING MINI-TEST 7, Question 2	SPEAKING COMPLETE TEST 1, Question 3	SPEAKING COMPLETE TEST 2, Question 3
	SKILL-ASSESSMENT CHECKLIST **Speaking Integrated Tasks, Reading and Listening: Skills 5–8**									
SKILL 5	I noted the **main points** of the **reading passage**.									
SKILL 6	I noted the **main points** of the **listening passage**.									
SKILL 7	I read the **question** carefully.									
SKILL 7	I included a topic statement and supporting ideas in my **plan**.									
SKILL 8	I began with an overall **topic statement**.									
SKILL 8	I used strong **supporting ideas**.									
SKILL 8	I used **transitions** to connect the supporting ideas.									

	SPEAKING DIAGNOSTIC PRE-TEST, Question 4	SPEAKING REVIEW EXERCISE (Skills 9–12)	SPEAKING POST-TEST, Question 4	SPEAKING MINI-TEST 2, Question 2	SPEAKING MINI-TEST 4, Question 2	SPEAKING MINI-TEST 6, Question 2	SPEAKING MINI-TEST 8, Question 2	SPEAKING COMPLETE TEST 1, Question 4	SPEAKING COMPLETE TEST 2, Question 4
SKILL-ASSESSMENT CHECKLIST **Speaking Integrated Tasks, Reading and Listening: Skills 9–12**									
SKILL 9 I noted the **main points** of the **reading passage**.									
SKILL 10 I noted the **main points** of the **listening passage**.									
SKILL 11 I read the **question** carefully.									
SKILL 11 I included a topic statement and supporting ideas in my **plan**.									
SKILL 12 I began with an overall **topic statement**.									
SKILL 12 I used strong **supporting ideas**.									
SKILL 12 I used **transitions** to connect the supporting ideas.									

	SKILL-ASSESSMENT CHECKLIST Speaking Integrated Tasks, Listening: Skills 13–15								
		SPEAKING DIAGNOSTIC PRE-TEST, Question 5	SPEAKING REVIEW EXERCISE (Skills 13–15)	SPEAKING POST-TEST, Question 5	SPEAKING MINI-TEST 2, Question 3	SPEAKING MINI-TEST 4, Question 3	SPEAKING MINI-TEST 6, Question 3	SPEAKING MINI-TEST 8, Question 3	SPEAKING COMPLETE TEST 1, Question 5	SPEAKING COMPLETE TEST 2, Question 5
SKILL 13	I noted the **main points** of the **listening passage**.									
SKILL 14	I read the **question** carefully.									
SKILL 14	I included a topic statement and key details in my **plan**.									
SKILL 15	I began with an overall **topic statement**.									
SKILL 15	I used **key details**.									
SKILL 15	I used **transitions** to connect the key details.									

SKILL-ASSESSMENT CHECKLIST
Speaking Integrated Tasks, Listening: Skills 16–18

	SPEAKING DIAGNOSTIC PRE-TEST, Question 6	SPEAKING REVIEW EXERCISE (Skills 16–18)	SPEAKING POST-TEST, Question 6	SPEAKING MINI-TEST 1, Question 3	SPEAKING MINI-TEST 3, Question 3	SPEAKING MINI-TEST 5, Question 3	SPEAKING MINI-TEST 7, Question 3	SPEAKING COMPLETE TEST 1, Question 6	SPEAKING COMPLETE TEST 2, Question 6
SKILL 16 I noted the **main points** of the **listening passage**.									
SKILL 17 I read the **question** carefully.									
SKILL 17 I included a topic statement and key details in my **plan**.									
SKILL 18 I began with an overall **topic statement**.									
SKILL 18 I used **key details**.									
SKILL 18 I used **transitions** to connect the key details.									

SCORING THE SPEAKING TESTS USING THE SCORING CRITERIA

You may use the Speaking Scoring Criteria to score your speaking tasks on the Pre-Test, Post-Test, Mini-Tests, and Complete Tests. You will receive a score of 0 through 4 for each Speaking task; this score of 0 through 4 will then be converted to a scaled score out of 30. The criteria for Speaking scores of 0 through 4 are listed below.

	SPEAKING SCORING CRITERIA	
4	ANSWER TO QUESTION	The student answers the question thoroughly.
	COMPREHENSIBILITY	The student can be understood completely.
	ORGANIZATION	The student's response is well organized and developed.
	FLUENCY	The student's speech is generally fluent.
	PRONUNCIATION	The student has generally good pronunciation.
	GRAMMAR	The student uses advanced grammatical structures with a high degree of accuracy.
	VOCABULARY	The student uses advanced vocabulary with a high degree of accuracy.
3	ANSWER TO QUESTION	The student answers the questions adequately but not thoroughly.
	COMPREHENSIBILITY	The student can generally be understood.
	ORGANIZATION	The student's response is organized basically and is not thoroughly developed.
	FLUENCY	The student's speech is generally fluent, with minor problems.
	PRONUNCIATION	The student has generally good pronunciation, with minor problems.
	GRAMMAR	The student uses either accurate easier grammatical structures or more advanced grammatical structures with some errors.
	VOCABULARY	The student uses either accurate easier vocabulary or more advanced vocabulary with some errors.

2	ANSWER TO QUESTION	The student discusses information from the task but does not answer the question directly.
	COMPREHENSIBILITY	The student is not always intelligible.
	ORGANIZATION	The student's response is not clearly organized and is incomplete or contains some inaccurate points.
	FLUENCY	The student's speech is not very fluent and has a number of problems.
	PRONUNCIATION	The student's pronunciation is not very clear, with a number of problems.
	GRAMMAR	The student has a number of errors in grammar or uses only very basic grammar fairly accurately.
	VOCABULARY	The student has a number of errors in vocabulary or uses only very basic vocabulary fairly accurately.
1	ANSWER TO QUESTION	The student's response is only slightly related to the topic.
	COMPREHENSIBILITY	The student is only occasionally intelligible.
	ORGANIZATION	The student's response is not clearly organized and is only minimally on the topic.
	FLUENCY	The student has problems with fluency that make the response difficult to understand.
	PRONUNCIATION	The student has problems with pronunciation that make the response difficult to understand.
	GRAMMAR	The student has numerous errors in grammar that interfere with meaning.
	VOCABULARY	The student has numerous errors in vocabulary that interfere with meaning.
0	The student either says nothing or fails to answer the question.	

The following chart shows how a score of 0 through 4 on a Speaking task is converted to a scaled score out of 30.

SPEAKING SCORE (0–4)	SPEAKING SCALED SCORE (0–30)
4.00	30
3.83	29
3.66	28
3.50	27
3.33	26
3.16	24
3.00	23
2.83	22
2.66	20
2.50	19
2.33	18
2.16	17
2.00	15
1.83	14
1.66	13
1.50	11
1.33	10
1.16	9
1.00	8
0.83	6
0.66	5
0.50	4
0.33	3
0.16	1
0.00	0

Scaled scores on each of the Speaking tasks on a test are averaged to determine the scaled score for the test.

RECORDING YOUR SPEAKING TEST RESULTS

Each time that you complete a Speaking Pre-Test, Speaking Post-Test, Speaking Mini-Test, or Speaking Complete Test section, you should record the results in the chart that follows. In this way, you will be able to keep track of the progress you are making.

SPEAKING TEST RESULTS	
SPEAKING PRE-TEST	Speaking Task 1 _____ Speaking Task 2 _____ Speaking Task 3 _____ Speaking Task 4 _____ Speaking Task 5 _____ Speaking Task 6 _____ **Overall Speaking Score** _____
SPEAKING POST-TEST	Speaking Task 1 _____ Speaking Task 2 _____ Speaking Task 3 _____ Speaking Task 4 _____ Speaking Task 5 _____ Speaking Task 6 _____ **Overall Speaking Score** _____
SPEAKING MINI-TEST 1	Speaking Task 1 _____ Speaking Task 2 _____ Speaking Task 3 _____ **Overall Speaking Score** _____
SPEAKING MINI-TEST 2	Speaking Task 1 _____ Speaking Task 2 _____ Speaking Task 3 _____ **Overall Speaking Score** _____
SPEAKING MINI-TEST 3	Speaking Task 1 _____ Speaking Task 2 _____ Speaking Task 3 _____ **Overall Speaking Score** _____
SPEAKING MINI-TEST 4	Speaking Task 1 _____ Speaking Task 2 _____ Speaking Task 3 _____ **Overall Speaking Score** _____

SPEAKING MINI-TEST 5	Speaking Task 1 _____ Speaking Task 2 _____ Speaking Task 3 _____ **Overall Speaking Score** _____
SPEAKING MINI-TEST 6	Speaking Task 1 _____ Speaking Task 2 _____ Speaking Task 3 _____ **Overall Speaking Score** _____
SPEAKING MINI-TEST 7	Speaking Task 1 _____ Speaking Task 2 _____ Speaking Task 3 _____ **Overall Speaking Score** _____
SPEAKING MINI-TEST 8	Speaking Task 1 _____ Speaking Task 2 _____ Speaking Task 3 _____ **Overall Speaking Score** _____
SPEAKING COMPLETE TEST 1	Speaking Task 1 _____ Speaking Task 2 _____ Speaking Task 3 _____ Speaking Task 4 _____ Speaking Task 5 _____ Speaking Task 6 _____ **Overall Speaking Score** _____
SPEAKING COMPLETE TEST 2	Speaking Task 1 _____ Speaking Task 2 _____ Speaking Task 3 _____ Speaking Task 4 _____ Speaking Task 5 _____ Speaking Task 6 _____ **Overall Speaking Score** _____

RECORDING SCRIPT

SPEAKING DIAGNOSTIC PRE-TEST

Page 3
Question 3

Listen to the passage. On a piece of paper, take notes on the main points of the listening passage.

(woman) You're going to take some classes in the Humanities Department next semester, aren't you, Paul?

(man) I'm taking two of them.

(woman) I think you're going to sign up for the same two I'm taking.

(man) Yeah, we both have the same two classes to take.

(woman) Have you gotten a signature yet?

(man) A signature? Whose signature do I have to get?

(woman) You have to get your advisor's signature so that you can register for the two humanities courses you want to take.

(man) Since when? I've never had to get a signature from my advisor to register for classes.

(woman) There's a new policy. I saw a notice on the door of the Humanities Department office.

(man) I haven't seen the notice. I'll have to go check it out . . . but it says that every student has to get an advisor's signature to register for any class?

(woman) To register for any class in the Humanities Department, any class except the introductory classes.

(man) I guess I'll have to go see my advisor.

(woman) Me, too.

(man) But first I'm going to go over to the Humanities Department and look at the notice. Listen, thanks for telling me about this.

HOW DOES THE STUDENTS' CONVERSATION ADD TO THE INFORMATION INCLUDED IN THE NOTICE?

Page 4
Question 4

Listen to the passage. On a piece of paper, take notes on the main points of the listening passage.

(professor) I'd like to make a couple of points, now, about nonverbal communication. The first point is that nonverbal communication does not require intent. One can communicate nonverbally without intending to do so. Think about a student who's feeling bored listening to a professor drone on and on; this student might not want to make his or her boredom clear to the professor, might not want to offend the professor, but perhaps the student's boredom is clear to anyone who looks at him or her.

Now, there's another point I'd like to make about nonverbal communication. This second point is that nonverbal communication doesn't take place automatically simply because one person has tried to communicate nonverbally. There has to be communication. If one person makes a certain gesture or expression, for example, but no one understands it, then no communication has taken place. There is communication only if the gesture or expression is understood.

HOW DOES THE PROFESSOR SUPPLEMENT THE INFORMATION INCLUDED IN THE READING?

Page 5
Question 5

Listen to the passage. On a piece of paper, take notes on the main points of the listening passage.

(woman) Hey, Mark, you're studying French, aren't you?

(man) No, I'm studying Spanish.

(woman) Spanish? Oh, I thought you were studying French, like me. I was going to ask you about some of the French courses.

(man) I don't know about French courses; I only know about Spanish courses, but I think the courses in the two departments are the same. What's your question? Maybe I can help.

(woman) My question's about the intermediate courses.

(man) I'm taking intermediate Spanish.

(woman) I'm enrolled in the intermediate French course, but it doesn't seem right for me.

(man) Why not? It's too easy?

(woman) (laughs) I wish. No, it's too hard.

(man) Did you study French in high school?

(woman) Yes, for three years. I had three years of French in high school.

(man) I had three years of Spanish in high school, and now I'm in the intermediate Spanish class, and it seems to be the right level for me.

(woman) I guess that answers my question. I must be in the class I'm supposed to be in. I had three years of French in high school, but intermediate French just seems too hard for me. I just can't believe that I might need to go back to beginning French when I studied three years of French in high school.

(man) What's the problem in your intermediate French class? Are you sure it's too hard for you?

(woman) The problem is that I don't understand anything in class, anything at all.

(man) Do the other students seem to understand better than you?

(woman) I don't know. I haven't really noticed.

(man) Maybe you should talk with the other students and see if they're having trouble understanding, too. That would help you know if you're in the right place . . . And maybe you should talk with the professor, too, and find out if he thinks . . .

(woman) She thinks. . . .

(man) OK, find out if she thinks you're in the right class.

(woman) So you think I should talk to the other students and to the professor?

(man) I do.

(woman) But not in French. That's too hard for me.

WHAT DOES THE MAN SUGGEST THE WOMAN SHOULD DO TO DEAL WITH THE PROBLEM SHE IS HAVING?

Page 5

Question 6

Listen to the passage. On a piece of paper, take notes on the main points of the listening passage.

(professor) Today, I'll be talking about whales, specifically about how whales use echolocation. Do you know what echolocation is? Well, in broad terms, it's a technique used by whales to determine what's going on in their surroundings. The term is "echolocation"; this term is composed of two ideas, "echo" and "location." Basically, echolocation refers to the technique of using echoes to determine the location of whatever is in the surrounding area.

I have a few points to make about echolocation. The first point is that it seems that only toothed whales can use echolocation. I'm sure you understand that some whales have teeth and others don't. It's only the toothed whales that seem to have this capability.

Next, I'd like to talk about what happens during echolocation. A whale uses echolocation by sending out a series of clicks. The clicks then bounce off objects in the water and are reflected back to the whale. So echolocation is actually a series of clicks sent out by a whale that bounce off objects and are then reflected back to the whale.

Now, what is it exactly that a whale can learn from these clicks that bounce off an object? Quite a bit, actually. A whale can learn the size and shape of objects that are out there. But that's not all. From the reflected clicks a whale can learn more than the size and shape of an object. It can also understand how far away the object is and if the object is moving, the

whale can understand how fast the object is moving and what direction it's moving.

WHAT POINTS DOES THE PROFESSOR MAKE ABOUT ECHOLOCATION?

SPEAKING EXERCISE 6

Page 25

1. Listen to the passage. On a piece of paper, take notes on the main points of the listening passage.

(man) Beth, you ride a bicycle to school, don't you?

(woman) Yes, I do.

(man) And I do, too. You saw the notice about bicycle parking?

(woman) What notice about bicycle parking?

(man) You didn't see it, then?

(woman) No, I didn't. What did it say?

(man) It said that we can't park our bicycles on campus near our classrooms.

(woman) What do you mean?

(man) The notice says that bicycles can be parked only along the east and west sides of campus, in the official bicycle parking locations.

(woman) And we can't leave our bicycles anywhere else on campus?

(man) No, we can't.

(woman) Well, what's going to happen if I leave my bicycle on campus, next to the building where I have class?

(man) If you leave your bicycle anywhere on campus except the authorized lots on the east and west sides of campus, you'll get a ticket.

(woman) Oh, no. That doesn't sound fair. I don't like that at all.

(man) You can say that again!

Page 25

2. Listen to the passage. On a piece of paper, take notes on the main points of the listening passage.

(man) Cathy, did you hear that Dr. Connor's retiring?

(woman) I certainly did. I can't believe it. It seems like she's been here forever.

(man) It's too bad she's leaving. I was hoping to take one of her classes.

(woman) Me, too. You know, my father took several classes from Dr. Connor.

(man) He did? You mean, he was a student here?

(woman) Yeah, he graduated from here 30 years ago.

(man) And he took classes from Dr. Connor when he was here?

(woman) That's right. He's told me how much he enjoyed her classes, so I really want to take at least one before she retires.

(man) Well, she'll only be here for one more semester before she retires, so that'll be your only chance to take one, and my only chance, too.

(woman) Then we really have to make sure to sign up for at least one of her classes for the spring semester, don't we?

(man) We sure do.

Page 26

3. Listen to the passage. On a piece of paper, take notes on the main points of the listening passage.

(man) Hey, Alice. Did you read the syllabus from Professor Thompson's class?

(woman) I looked it over.

(man) Well, did you see the part about the assignments?

(woman) You mean the part describing the assignments, what we have to do for each assignment?

(man) No, I mean the part about the due dates for the assignments.

(woman) Oh, you mean the part about late assignments, about how the professor doesn't like late assignments?

(man) Yeah, that part. It seems kind of strict, doesn't it? You don't think he actually means it, do you, that he won't accept any late assignments even if we're sick?

(woman) Actually, I'm quite sure he does mean it, absolutely.

(man) Why are you so sure of that?

(woman) Because that's how he's always been, from what I know. I heard about a student who was in his class, and this student was in an accident on his bicycle, one that wasn't his fault, and he was in the hospital. He'd even broken his arm and couldn't write, and Professor Thompson wouldn't even accept any late papers from him.

(man) Not even from a guy who was in the hospital with a broken arm and couldn't write because of the broken arm?

(woman) Not even from him.

(man) Well, then, I guess Professor Thompson's pretty serious about the policy on late papers.

(woman) He certainly is.

SPEAKING REVIEW EXERCISE (Skills 5 through 8)

Page 30

Listen to the passage. On a piece of paper, take notes on the main points of the listening passage.

(woman) Do you understand the assignment for the research project in our history class?

(man) I think so.

(woman) Well, I'm not quite sure what the assignment is. What do you think we're supposed to do?

(man) Well, we're supposed to choose one event or person and research that event or person and then write about it from positive and negative perspectives.

(woman) That's what I thought the syllabus said, but it seems strange. Why do you think the professor wants us to do this?

(man) I don't know for sure, but I can think of two reasons why he might.

(woman) What are they?

(man) Number one, I think he wants to get across to us that research involves a number of sources, not just one.

(woman) Yeah, it seems easier to look at just one source, but I understand that we need to look in several sources. That makes sense. Now, what's your second reason?

(man) Number two, I think the professor wants to get across that a single event can be viewed in different ways. Think of someone like Columbus. In some accounts he's viewed as a hero, while in other accounts he's viewed as a villain.

(woman) OK, that makes sense. Now all I need is a good topic. It sounds like maybe you already have yours.

HOW DOES THE INFORMATION IN THE LISTENING PASSAGE ADD TO THE INFORMATION IN THE READING PASSAGE?

SPEAKING EXERCISE 10

Page 34

1. Listen to the passage. On a piece of paper, take notes on the main points of the listening passage.

(professor) An interesting point that I'd like to add about the body of water called the Dead Sea is that it's not actually a sea but is instead a lake, a rather large lake, but a lake, not a sea. A sea refers to either a division of the ocean or to a large body of water that's partially, but not entirely, enclosed by land, one that opens into an ocean; a lake is a body of water that's entirely enclosed. The North Sea, for example, is a sea because it's a section of the northeastern part of the Atlantic Ocean, and the Mediterranean is a sea because it opens into the Atlantic. Because the Dead Sea is landlocked with no outlet, it's a lake rather than a sea.

Page 35

2. Listen to the passage. On a piece of paper, take notes on the main points of the listening passage.

(professor) Now I'd like to discuss one particular type of polling, a negative and unfair type of polling known as push polling. Push polling involves trying to plant negative information under the guise of conducting an opinion poll. By this, I mean that a pollster tells someone that he simply wants to ask the person's opinion and then, instead of merely finding out that person's opinion, tries to surreptitiously implant negative information in the person's mind. A pollster who uses the technique of push polling may call a potential voter who supports candidate X not to find out which candidate the voter supports but to implant negative information about candidate X in the voter's mind. The pollster might ask leading questions such as "Would you support candidate X if you knew that he spent time in prison?" or "Would you support candidate X if you knew he had a problem with alcohol?" The questions asked by a pollster who is push polling are designed more to implant negative information than to find out how the voter actually feels.

Page 35

3. Listen to the passage. On a piece of paper, take notes on the main points of the listening passage.

(professor) I'd like to talk about something that the Polynesians may have done in their travels. It seems quite possible that the Polynesians actually made it all the way to South America in their travels, and this seems quite astounding when you consider that they were traveling on outrigger canoes made of only two tree trunks and a platform. There are a number of indications that the Polynesians may have traveled all the way to South America. One important piece of information that leads historians to believe that the Polynesians made it to South America is that there were plants from South America in Hawaii when Europeans first arrived in Hawaii. How did these plants from South America get to Hawaii before the Europeans arrived there? Quite possibly it was the Polynesians who carried the plants from South America to the Hawaiian Islands in their outrigger canoes.

SPEAKING REVIEW EXERCISE (Skills 9 through 12)

Page 39

Listen to the passage. On a piece of paper, take notes on the main points of the listening passage.

(professor) Let's look at a couple of situations to see the equity theory in action. We'll talk about this theory in terms of a mythical employee, employee X.

In the first situation, a coworker of employee X has the same job title as employee X, does the same amount of work, makes the same amount of money, and has a similar office. In this situation, employee X will feel satisfied with his job because he and his coworker receive equal returns for their contributions.

The second situation is different. In the second situation, a coworker of employee X has the same job title but does less work, makes more money, and has a bigger office than employee X. In this situation, employee X will not feel

satisfied because he receives a lower return for his contribution than the coworker.

HOW DOES THE INFORMATION IN THE LISTENING PASSAGE ADD TO THE INFORMATION IN THE READING PASSAGE?

SPEAKING EXERCISE 13

Page 42

1. Listen to the passage. On a piece of paper, take notes on the main points of the listening passage.

(man) Hey there, how are you doing?
(woman) Oh, just fine, thanks. Listen, can I ask you a question?
(man) Sure. About what?
(woman) About the course Cultural History of the United States.
(man) Oh, yeah, that's a great class. I took it last year.
(woman) And you really enjoyed it?
(man) I did. I took it with Dr. Abbott. I really enjoyed his course.
(woman) I'm glad. Listen, I saw that two different professors are teaching the course next quarter, and I was wondering if you could recommend one of them. It sounds like you enjoyed Dr. Abbott's course and would recommend him.
(man) I did enjoy Dr. Abbott's class, but . . . well . . . it's not for everyone.
(woman) What do you mean, that it's not for everyone?
(man) Oh, I really enjoyed it, but not everyone did.
(woman) Why not?
(man) In Dr. Abbott's course, we didn't need to memorize a lot of details.
(woman) That sounds good.
(man) And there was a lot of interesting discussion.
(woman) That sounds good, too. Why were some of the students unhappy with the course?
(man) It was the exams. The exams were all essay exams. Some people didn't like that.
(woman) Yeah, I probably wouldn't like that either. . . . By the way, do you know anything about the other professor who teaches the same course, Dr. Becker? Do you know anything about Dr. Becker's course? Is it just like Dr. Abbott's course?
(man) I've heard it's really different. Dr. Becker's a lot more concerned about details; she really concentrates on the details.
(woman) Do you know what her exams are like? Are they essay exams, like Dr. Abbott's?
(man) I've heard that her exams are all multiple choice; there aren't any essays.
(woman) That part of it sounds good to me, but memorizing a lot of details doesn't. The lively discussion in Dr. Abbott's course also sounds good, but the essay exams don't. I've got to think about this some more

before I make a decision, but thanks for your help.

Page 42

2. Listen to the passage. On a piece of paper, take notes on the main points of the listening passage.

(woman) Hey, Alan, are you going to the game tonight?

(man) Oh, I can't, Anne, I have an exam on Friday, and I need to study for it.

(woman) It's too bad you're going to miss the game. It's going to be a great one. . . . You should've studied earlier so that you could go to the game, you know.

(man) I wish I had, but I didn't, and now I've got to spend tonight and tomorrow reviewing my notes.

(woman) It takes that much time for you to review your notes?

(man) I know it shouldn't take that much time, but it does.

(woman) Why does it, do you think?

(man) Well, when I'm in class, I think I take really good notes, I mean, I think I understand what the professor's talking about and I write down lots of stuff . . . it all makes sense at the time. But then it's usually a few weeks until there's an exam, and when I go back to my notes from a few weeks earlier, the notes don't make any sense. That's why it takes so much time for me to review my notes. The notes from a few weeks ago, the ones that I thought were so good, just don't make sense after a few weeks, so it takes a lot of time to sort them out. You see what my problem is?

(woman) I think I understand what your problem is, and, even better, I think I know what you could do to solve the problem.

(man) You do? What?

(woman) I think the most important thing I do, right after I take notes during a lecture, is to go over the notes and reorganize them.

(man) Really? You do that?

(woman) I do. I think that one of the most important things my high school advisor told me about university studies, and about lecture notes in particular, was to "never let them get cold." What she meant was that you shouldn't just take notes during class and forget about the notes for a while until the last minute before an exam. Instead, you should review the notes within a day or so, review them and organize them, if necessary.

(man) Is that what you do?

(woman) Yes, and it saves me so much time because it's much easier to prepare for exams this way.

(man) I guess it can't hurt me to give it a try with the lectures that are coming up, but right now I need to go prepare for the exam on Friday.

(woman) So you can't go to the game?

(man) I really do wish I could, but I can't.

Page 43

3. Listen to the passage. On a piece of paper, take notes on the main points of the listening passage.

(woman) Hi, Mike, do you have a moment? I'd like to talk with you about something.

(man) Sure, Nicky. I have a few minutes before I have to head over to my next class. What's your question?

(woman) It's about independent study, about an independent study project with Dr. Lee. You did an independent study project last year, and you did your project with Dr. Lee, didn't you?

(man) I sure did. You have a question about that?

(woman) I do. I'd like to know what it's like. I mean, how to do a good job of it.

(man) Uh . . . maybe I'm not the best person to talk about this because I . . . uh . . . didn't do a very good job on my project, I don't think.

(woman) (laughs) Well, then, maybe you can talk with me about what <u>not</u> to do, how <u>not</u> to do a project.

(man) Now that's my area of expertise. I can tell you about what you shouldn't do . . . OK, well first of all, and most important, you need to work on your project regularly. You'll only have meetings with Dr. Lee once a month. What I did was, uh, to not do any work on my project for about three and a half weeks each month, and then I'd spend a couple of days just before meeting with Dr. Lee working on nothing but my project.

(woman) That certainly doesn't sound like the best way to do a project like this. I need to work on the project throughout each month before I meet with Dr. Lee instead of putting all the work off until the last few days of each month. That makes sense . . . OK, what else can you tell me to help me with the project? Or what else can you tell me <u>not</u> to do?

(man) Let's see . . . OK, something else you should keep in mind, and I had trouble with this, too, when I was working on my project, is that it's an <u>independent</u> study project.

(woman) So it means that you work on the project independently?

(man) It also means that <u>you</u> determine the direction your research will take; Dr. Lee doesn't do that.

(woman) What do you mean exactly?

(man) Well, I kept expecting Dr. Lee to tell me what I should do next, but he expected me to figure out what I should do and then discuss it with him.

(woman) Oh, I see now. I need to take charge of figuring out the direction the project should take and not expect Dr. Lee to do that.

(man) Exactly. Think about these things if you decide to work on an independent study project with Dr. Lee. Then you should be able to do a much better job than I did.

SPEAKING REVIEW EXERCISE (Skills 13 through 15)

Page 47

Listen to the passage. On a piece of paper, take notes on the main points of the listening passage.

(woman) Are you enjoying Professor Taylor's class?

(man) Not exactly.

(woman) Why not? Why don't you like it?

(man) Well, I get bored in class. It's a two-hour class twice a week, and usually within 15 minutes of the start of the class, I'm nodding off, and it's really hard for me to keep my head up and try to keep my eyes open for the next two hours. One of these days I'm going to fall asleep outright and start snoring out loud right in the middle of class.

(woman) Well, maybe you need to get involved in the class. If you're involved in the class, you can't possibly fall asleep.

(man) But how do I do that?

(woman) Um, let me think about it. . . . Let's see, how many students are in your class?

(man) It's a big class, there are about sixty students in a large classroom.

(woman) Where do you sit?

(man) I sit in the back because I always start falling asleep.

(woman) Well, sit in the front of the classroom, sit right up in the front. It's too easy to let your mind wander when you're in the back of the classroom, and you need to be involved in the class. So you should sit right up at the front of the classroom, close to the professor.

(man) OK, I can try sitting in the front and hope that I don't fall asleep right under the professor's nose. Now, do you have anything else to suggest?

(woman) Well, does the professor just lecture, or does he talk with the students, ask the students questions or answer questions from the students?

(man) He lectures mostly, but sometimes he asks questions, and he'll always answer questions if the students ask.

(woman) Do you ever answer any questions the professor asks?

(man) No, I can't because I'm usually sitting in the back of the room.

(woman) Well, then sit in the front and answer questions the professor asks. . . . Now, have you ever asked the professor a question in class?

(man) No.

(woman) Not ever?

(man) No, not ever.

(woman) Well, ask questions. Sit in the front of the classroom and ask questions. No wonder you're not involved in the class. You can take steps to get yourself involved in the class, and then you just might begin to enjoy it a whole lot.

WHAT DOES THE WOMAN SUGGEST THE MAN CAN DO TO DEAL WITH HIS PROBLEM?

SPEAKING EXERCISE 16

Page 49

1. Listen to the passage. On a piece of paper, take notes on the main points of the listening passage.

(professor) Today we're going to be talking about the Bank Holiday of 1933. A holiday. A bank holiday. Sounds like a nice thing, doesn't it? But it really wasn't. It occurred when the U.S. banking system was in serious trouble in 1933, but somehow this situation became known as a holiday rather than as a disaster.

Let's talk about what led up to the Bank Holiday of 1933. In the 1920s, banking in the United States hadn't been very stable, and it wasn't unusual for banks to fail. Then, after the stock market crashed in 1929, the problem with banks became much worse. By 1933, more than half the states had closed banks.

The solution to this problem was when President Roosevelt called a bank holiday. This bank holiday meant that all banks were closed for a period of days while the federal government worked to reorganize the banking system. One of the bills passed by the government at the time was federal deposit insurance, which means that any money deposited in U.S. banks would be insured by the federal government.

Since the time of the bank holiday, the situation has improved considerably. The number of banks that fail has decreased sharply, and the number of people to lose money by depositing it in a federally insured account has remained at zero.

Page 50

2. Listen to the passage. On a piece of paper, take notes on the main points of the listening passage.

(professor) Today we're going to talk about creativity. Think about it for a moment. What is creativity? How would you define creativity? It's kind of difficult, isn't it?

Let's look at what the experts have to say about this. Rather than actually defining creativity, experts try to list what characteristics are part of creativity. Many researchers have studied creativity and have come up with lists of characteristics that their research has shown to be part of creativity. Unfortunately, as I'm sure you understand, various researchers are not in complete agreement as to what actually constitutes creativity.

There are, however, two characteristics that are widely accepted in research as being constituent parts of creativity. These two components of creativity are originality and appropriateness. Let's think about these two components of creativity, originality and appropriateness, in terms of a problem you need to solve, a problem that requires a creative solution. Can you see how originality and appropriateness would be part of a creative solution?

First, let's think about originality. If you need a creative solution to a problem, the solution you need isn't the normal, everyday solution that everyone comes up with. It must be an original solution, something new, something different.

Now let's think about appropriateness, when you're looking for a solution to a problem, it has to be an appropriate solution, doesn't it? If you suggest a solution to a problem but the solution isn't appropriate, say it can't be used because it will offend people or it won't solve the problem because it doesn't fit the problem, this isn't a good solution.

Thus, we've seen that for an idea to be creative, it has to, minimally, be original and appropriate. There may be other component parts to creativity, but originality and appropriateness are certainly part of it.

Page 50

3. Listen to the passage. On a piece of paper, take notes on the main points of the listening passage.

(professor) Have you ever wondered why the huge river in South America is called the Amazon? Well, two sources seem to have contributed to this name. One of these two sources for the modern name of the river is the original native name for the river, and the other source is a chronicle written when Europeans first explored the river in the sixteenth century.

The native inhabitants living near the giant river certainly must've contributed in part to the modern name of this river. The name given by the native inhabitants to this large river was something like the modern name. The native inhabitants called the river *Amazunu*, which in their language meant "big wave." I'm sure you can hear the similarity between the native name *Amazunu* and today's modern name Amazon.

However, today's modern name didn't come entirely from the native name for the river; there was another important source for the name Amazon, and this source comes from a sixteenth-century chronicle of the European exploration of the river. In early Greek literature, there were descriptions of a society of brave female warriors called Amazons. When the Europeans were exploring the river in the sixteenth century, a chronicle of the trip was kept. This chronicle of the exploration of the river in the

sixteenth century contains descriptions of courageous female warriors much like the female warriors described in ancient Greek literature. The chronicler made reference to the Amazon-like warriors on the river called Amazunu by the natives, which both helped to contribute to the river's modern name Amazon.

SPEAKING REVIEW EXERCISE (Skills 16 through 18)

Page 54

Listen to the passage. On a piece of paper, take notes on the main points of the listening passage.

(professor) Something that affects some residents of Alaska and other societies in the far north of the globe during the winter months is a disorder call SAD. SAD is actually an acronym S-A-D, and it stands for seasonal affective disorder. "S" for seasonal, "A" for affective, and "D" for disorder.

In the summertime, Alaska is blessed with a tremendous amount of sunshine, 20 hours of sunshine a day in Anchorage and 22 hours of sunshine a day in Fairbanks. In the winter, however, the opposite occurs, and there are long, long hours of darkness and only an occasional few hours of sunshine if the sky during the hours when sunshine is possible isn't cloudy or stormy.

During these long periods of darkness interrupted by little or no sunlight, residents can be afflicted by SAD, or seasonal affective disorder, a serious kind of clinical depression. Estimates of the percentage affected by SAD range from 10 to 20 percent of the population.

There's actually a physiological cause of this disorder, one that's related to the lack of regular sunlight. When the human body receives less sunlight, it produces less serotonin and more melatonin than usual. Serotonin is a hormone that causes humans to feel cheerful and positive, and less serotonin is produced when there's inadequate sunlight. Melatonin is a hormone that causes humans to feel drowsy and fall asleep, and more melatonin is produced when there's inadequate sunlight. It's this combination of reduced serotonin and increased melatonin that's the cause of seasonal affective disorder in areas where sunlight is reduced considerably for several months at a time.

WHAT POINTS DOES THE PROFESSOR MAKE ABOUT SAD?

SPEAKING POST-TEST

Page 57
Question 3

Listen to the passage. On a piece of paper, take notes on the main points of the listening passage.

(man)   Hey, Sue, are you heading over to the snack bar?

(woman) Yes, I am. So you heard that the main cafeteria's closed?

(man)   I didn't <u>hear</u> about it. I read the notice.

(woman) There's a notice about the main cafeteria being closed?

(man)   Yeah, there is. It's posted on the door of the main cafeteria. I went over to the cafeteria for lunch, and I read the notice, so now I'm going to one of the snack bars.

(woman) Sorry you had to walk all the way over there for nothing. I heard about the cafeteria being closed from one of the students in my class, so I didn't have to walk all the way over there for nothing.

(man)   Listen, do you know why the cafeteria's closed? I can't believe it's closed during the semester.

(woman) I heard there was a fire. Some people were in there cooking this morning, and a fire got started.

(man)   That would explain why the cafeteria's closed.

HOW DOES THE INFORMATION IN THE LISTENING PASSAGE ADD TO THE INFORMATION IN THE READING PASSAGE?

Page 58
Question 4

Listen to the passage. On a piece of paper, take notes on the main points of the listening passage.

(professor) As a teacher, it's important for you to recognize that you can take steps to establish the appropriate kind of social environment to meet the goals of each activity. It's not enough to recognize that certain types of social environments can exist in the classroom; it's also necessary to understand that you can take steps to ensure that the social environment is appropriate for a particular activity. To establish a cooperative environment, your role is to get across to the students that a particular task is to be completed in pairs or in groups and that only those responses that have been agreed upon by the entire group will be accepted. To establish a competitive environment, your role is to get across to the students that they must work alone and that their responses will be evaluated in comparison with responses from other students. To establish an individualistic environment, your role is to get across to the students that they are to work alone and that they are to do the best job they can and

that they'll be evaluated based upon a predetermined scale rather than on how well they do in comparison with other students.

HOW DOES THE INFORMATION IN THE LISTENING PASSAGE SUPPLEMENT THE INFORMATION IN THE READING PASSAGE?

Page 59
Question 5

Listen to the passage. On a piece of paper, take notes on the main points of the listening passage.

(man)   Hey, Beth. I saw you running across campus this morning. What was the hurry?

(woman) Oh, hi, Todd. I do that every morning I'm on campus. This morning was nothing unusual.

(man)   You go running across the campus every morning just for fun?

(woman) Oh, I'm not running for fun. I have to do that. It's the only way I can get to class on time.

(man)   You have two classes in a row that are on opposite sides of the campus?

(woman) Oh, it's much worse than that. I have <u>four</u> classes in a row, and I seem to have managed to choose four classes with one in each of the four corners of campus. So every day I end up running from the first class to the second, and from the second class to the third, and from the third class to the last one.

(man)   Why on earth did you schedule your classes that way?

(woman) It sounded like a good idea when I scheduled my classes. I thought it was a good idea to bunch my classes together. I have classes at eight o'clock in the morning, at nine o'clock, ten o'clock, and at eleven o'clock Monday through Thursday. It means that I'm finished with all of my classes by noon.

(man)   But it's not working out for you, is it?

(woman) No, it's not. I can't get from one class to the next without running because the classes are so far apart. And even though I move pretty quickly from class to class, I'm still usually late to each class. Here I thought I was making such a great schedule for myself when I selected these classes. I mean, it does sound nice to have all of my classes in the morning four days a week, doesn't it?

(man)   That part of it sounds good. It would be nice to have afternoons and evenings free . . . but the part where the classes are so far apart and you have to run from class to class and you're still late all of the time, that part doesn't sound so good.

(woman) It's not, I can assure you.

(man)   Maybe next semester you need to consider <u>where</u> your classes meet and not just <u>when</u> they meet.

(woman) That absolutely makes sense to me.

HOW DOES THE MAN FEEL ABOUT THE PROBLEM THE WOMAN HAS?

Page 59
Question 6

Listen to the passage. On a piece of paper, take notes on the main points of the listening passage.

(professor) Today we're going to talk about the planet Mars and, in particular, how people got the notion that Mars was inhabited by intelligent beings. We know today that there are no English-speaking humanlike beings with intelligence superior to ours populating the planet, but for quite some time people believed that there were. Where did this idea come from? Do you know?

As often happens, we'll see that the idea that there might be humanlike inhabitants on Mars at least in part was based on an error, a linguistic error of sorts. This linguistic error has to do with the word *canali* in Italian.

In 1877 an Italian astronomer was looking through a telescope at Mars, and he saw what looked like thin, straight lines on its surface. He called these faint lines *canali*. In Italian the word *canali* can refer to either something natural or something man-made. In English, however, a canal is something man-made, and a channel is something natural; a canal is man-made, as in the Erie Canal, while a channel is a natural depression, as in the English Channel. When the Italian astronomer called the lines on Mars *canali*, he most likely meant natural geographic features. However, when the word *canali* was translated into English, it was translated as "canal." From this, it was understood that astronomers were saying that there were features that had been <u>constructed</u> on Mars. If the features had been constructed, then the obvious conclusion would be that there were living beings on Mars who constructed the canals. Unfortunately, that wasn't what the astronomer meant; the astronomer was describing natural features on Mars rather than constructed ones.

WHAT POINTS DOES THE PROFESSOR MAKE ABOUT THE PLANET MARS?

SPEAKING MINI-TEST 1

Page 61
Question 2

Listen to the passage. On a piece of paper, take notes on the main points of the listening passage.

(woman) Isn't that a great assignment for history class?

(man) Which assignment?

(woman) The assignment where we have to watch a lot of films.

(man) I don't know. It seems like it's going to take a lot of time.

(woman) But we'll be spending time watching films.

(man) Watching films <u>and</u> writing reports. We have to write a report for each film we watch, you know.

(woman) I know we do, but we just have to write a report summarizing the key points of each film. We don't have to research anything, and we don't have to analyze anything. We can just summarize the main points of each film, and that really shouldn't take too much time at all.

(man) You've got a point there, . . . and I guess watching films is a better assignment than most assignments the professor could give. . . . I guess I'll have to get to work on watching those twelve films.

(woman) Only twelve? I'm going to try and watch all twenty.

(man) But we only have to watch twelve of them, right?

(woman) Yes, but we can watch more than twelve for extra credit, and I think watching films is a great way to earn some extra credit.

HOW DO THE STUDENTS SEEM TO FEEL ABOUT THE HISTORY CLASS ASSIGNMENT?

Page 62
Question 3

Listen to the passage. On a piece of paper, take notes on the main points of the listening passage.

(professor) Today, I'll be talking about glaciers and, in particular, how glaciers are formed. First of all, do you know what a glacier is? Well, a glacier is a mass of ice, but there's more to it than that. A glacier is a mass of ice that's <u>moving</u>.

Glaciers form where snow accumulates, where more snow falls than melts, so it piles up. If all the snow melts every year in a particular place, a glacier can't form there. And there needs to be considerable accumulation. If there's only a small amount of accumulation, then a glacier can't form because there needs to be considerable weight for a glacier to form, so there must be enough accumulation of sufficient weight for a glacier to form.

When enough snow has accumulated, there's pressure on the snow underneath, enough pressure to transform the loose snowflakes into ice crystals. The weight of the accumulated snow causes the snowflakes to compress into ice crystals. And with more and more pressure, the smaller ice crystals pack together to create even larger crystals.

The final step in the formation of a glacier is for the packed ice to begin to move. When the amount of crystallized ice becomes large enough, the packed ice begins to move and a glacier is born.

HOW ARE GLACIERS FORMED?

SPEAKING MINI-TEST 2

Page 64

Question 2

Listen to the passage. On a piece of paper, take notes on the main points of the listening passage.

(professor)   In a certain company, work was completed in work groups. Each employee was assigned to a work group, and each employee was evaluated, not on individual work, but on the quality of the work of his or her group. Two of the work groups in the company had very different leaders.

In the first group, the leader started off each group meeting with an activity designed to help the group members get to know each other. The leader then had the group members each make a positive comment about how the work on the group project was going. The leader ended each meeting by asking group members to send him an e-mail describing how they felt that the meeting had gone.

Work in the second group was very different. The group leader in the second group prepared a detailed list of what each group member was to get done in the following week. In each weekly meeting, the group leader grilled each group member about what he or she had and had not managed to accomplish since the last meeting and made it clear that the work on the list needed to be completed on time.

HOW DOES THE INFORMATION IN THE LISTENING PASSAGE ADD TO THE INFORMATION IN THE READING PASSAGE?

Page 65

Question 3

Listen to the passage. On a piece of paper, take notes on the main points of the listening passage.

(woman)   Are you going to the meeting tonight, Jeff?
(man)   Which meeting?
(woman)   The student council meeting.
(man)   Oh, the open meeting, the one where any students can attend?
(woman)   Yeah, that meeting.
(man)   I don't think I'm going.
(woman)   Why not? Didn't you want to take part in the discussion about the exam schedule?
(man)   I'm happy with the exam schedule as it is. I like having a six-day final exam schedule.

(woman)   But that's why you need to go to the meeting.
(man)   What do you mean?
(woman)   Well, the student council's holding an open meeting to discuss changing the final exam schedule, and a lot of students want to change the schedule. I think a lot of students who want to change the exam schedule will be at the open meeting this evening.
(man)   You mean, if I want the final exam schedule to stay just like it is, then I need to go to the meeting to support the idea of keeping the schedule just like it is?
(woman)   That's right. That's why I'm going.
(man)   You mean, you don't want the schedule to change?
(woman)   No way. You know how they're considering changing the schedule?
(man)   They want to shorten it a little bit, don't they?
(woman)   They want to shorten it a lot. They want to cut it in half.
(man)   You mean, they want to reduce the final exam schedule from six days to three days?
(woman)   That's right.
(man)   But I have five final exams. If my five exams are spread out over six days, then I'll be OK, but if I have five exams in three days, I'm going to have a really hard time.
(woman)   Me, too. I have five final exams, too.
(man)   But why would anyone want to reduce the exam schedule from six to three days?
(woman)   So that summer vacation will start three says earlier.
(man)   But it would make the final exam schedule really horrible.
(woman)   That's why we need to go to that meeting tonight, to try and keep the exam schedule just like it is.
(man)   OK, you've convinced me. I'll be there.
(woman)   So will I.

HOW DO THE STUDENTS SEEM TO FEEL ABOUT WHAT WILL BE DISCUSSED AT THE STUDENT COUNCIL MEETING?

SPEAKING MINI-TEST 3

Page 67

Question 2

Listen to the passage. On a piece of paper, take notes on the main points of the listening passage.

(man)   Boy, that notice is terrible!
(woman)   You really think so? I kind of like it. I mean, I really like it.
(man)   But it means we can't do anything in the library.
(woman)   Not exactly. We can study, we can do homework, we can work on research, and we can do all of these things in peace and quiet.
(man)   But so many of the students, myself included, like to talk to friends, maybe

have a little snack, take a little nap if we get
tired, play a little music to relax.

(woman) I know. That's why students like me can't
get any work done in the library.

(man) I like to get <u>some</u> work done in the library,
but I can't work all the time.

(woman) Well, I'm glad this notice was posted, and
now I only hope that it's enforced.

(man) If it is, I may have to go somewhere else to
work.

(woman) *(laughs)* It's not the work that's the
problem. It's the noise and the mess. I'm
really glad something's finally getting done
about this.

**HOW DO THE STUDENTS REACT TO THE NOTICE
POSTED IN THE LIBRARY?**

Page 68
Question 3

Listen to the passage. On a piece of paper, take notes on
the main points of the listening passage.

(professor) I'd like to talk today about some of the
formal grammar rules in English, rules
about what's considered formally correct
and incorrect. I'd like to talk in particular
about rules that were formed in the
seventeenth and eighteenth centuries
during the period of neoclassicism.

During the seventeenth and eighteenth
centuries in Europe, there was a widely
held view that the culture of ancient
Greece and Rome was superior to the
culture of the day. This period in the
seventeenth and eighteenth century is
known as the neoclassic period.

During the neoclassic period, academics
held the view that the Latin language of
the classic age of the Roman Empire was
the purest language possible; as a result,
there was an attempt to Latinize the
English of the time to make it resemble
what was considered the most perfect
language, Latin.

An example of a formal grammar rule
that developed in English during the
neoclassic revival is the rule against
split infinitives. The infinitive is the
form of the verb that includes the word
"to" and the base form of the verb, such
as "to go," or "to walk," or "to make."
There is a formal rule today in English
against splitting the infinitive, against
saying something like "to never go," or
"to always work," or "to usually finish,"
though many native speakers of English
do break this formal rule fairly often.

This formal rule against split infinitives
did not exist before the neoclassic period.
Instead, it came about as seventeenth
and eighteenth century academics during
the neoclassic period noted that it's
impossible to split infinitives in Latin;
it's impossible to split infinitives in Latin

because a Latin verb is one word rather
than the two words that make up an
English infinitive. However, because
infinitives were never split in Latin, the
rule against splitting infinitives was
created. English speakers still, however,
regularly split their infinitives; the
attempt by seventeenth and eighteenth
century academics to impose a rule
against split infinitives in order to make
English more like Latin did not succeed
entirely.

**WHY DOES THE PROFESSOR USE THE EXAMPLE
OF SPLIT INFINITIVES?**

SPEAKING MINI-TEST 4

Page 70
Question 2

Listen to the passage. On a piece of paper, take notes on
the main points of the listening passage.

(professor) The issue of nullification caused a serious
controversy in one particular situation in
the first part of the nineteenth century.
In 1828, the U.S. Congress passed a bill
that authorized new tariffs on some
imported manufactured goods. This
meant that taxes would have to be paid
to the federal government when certain
manufactured goods were imported, and
since many goods were not manufactured
in the United States at the time, if people
wanted to have these goods, then the
goods had to be imported.

The issue of nullification arose in this
situation when one of the southern states
in the United States held a convention
to discuss the tariffs on some imported
products; the convention voted to nullify
the law that required that tariffs be paid
on those imported goods. In other words,
the state voted not to follow a law passed
by the federal government.

The president of the United States,
Andrew Jackson, sent federal troops into
the state to impose the federal law on
tariffs there. A compromise was reached
when the government passed a new law
that lowered the tariff, and the southern
state agreed to pay this lower tariff.

**HOW DOES THE INFORMATION IN THE
LISTENING PASSAGE ADD TO WHAT IS
EXPLAINED IN THE READING PASSAGE?**

Page 71
Question 3

Listen to the passage. On a piece of paper, take notes on
the main points of the listening passage.

(woman) Hey, Steve, can I ask you something?
(man) Sure, Chris, what do you want to know?
(woman) It's about the paper in our psychology class.

(man)	The one for next week?
(woman)	No, the first one we did. The one we got back in class today.
(man)	Oh, that one. What do you want to know about it?
(woman)	You seem to have done a good job on it. I mean, the professor certainly complimented you on it when she returned it to you.
(man)	Oh, you heard what the professor said? That was kind of embarrassing.
(woman)	You shouldn't be embarrassed. The professor said you did a nice job on the paper. . . . Listen, I was wondering if you could help me a little, I mean, give me an idea about what you did that the professor liked.
(man)	I'm sure the professor liked your paper, too.
(woman)	Uh . . . no she didn't like it. The only comment she wrote on my paper was "Needs work." I don't think she liked it very much.
(man)	Well, I didn't do anything special. I mean, I just read the question she asked and wrote a very simple and direct answer to the question.
(woman)	You don't think she wanted something creative? I worked really hard to come up with a creative answer. I sort of told a story that indirectly implied my answer to the question.
(man)	You did? Really? Well, it sounds like the professor didn't appreciate the effort you put into your paper to make such a creative response.
(woman)	So you just wrote a simple answer?
(man)	A really simple, direct answer.
(woman)	And the professor certainly seemed to like that.
(man)	I guess so.
(woman)	Then I'll have to try that on the next paper. And here I was working so hard to try to think of a creative way to write the next paper.
(man)	I guess you don't need to do that.
(woman)	Not if I want to write a paper the professor likes . . . and I do.

WHAT IS HAPPENING WITH THE STUDENTS'
ASSIGNMENTS FOR THEIR PSYCHOLOGY
CLASS?

SPEAKING MINI-TEST 5

Page 73
Question 2

Listen to the passage. On a piece of paper, take notes on
the main points of the listening passage.

(woman)	Have you seen the notice about the positions in the Administration Building?
(man)	Yeah, I have, but I can't apply for them because of the requirements.
(woman)	Well, I'm going to apply for one of the positions.

(man)	But look at the requirements for the positions. The notice says that you need to have completed sixty units.
(woman)	I've finished forty-five. That should be enough.
(man)	And is your grade-point average 3.0 or higher? The notice says that a 3 point average is required.
(woman)	My grade-point average is 2.5. I'm sure that's close enough.
(man)	And what about your availability? The notice says you have to be free either in the mornings or in the afternoons, and I know you have at least one class in the morning and one in the afternoon.
(woman)	I'm sure that won't be a problem either. And the notice says that good computer and telephone skills are required, and I have both.
(man)	You may have good telephone skills, but you're always having to ask me for help with your computer. I think you're wasting your time thinking about these positions.
(woman)	I think this job sounds perfect for me. I've already submitted my application.

HOW DO THE STUDENTS RESPOND TO THE
NOTICE ABOUT THE POSITIONS IN THE
ADMINISTRATION BUILDING?

Page 74
Question 3

Listen to the passage. On a piece of paper, take notes on
the main points of the listening passage.

(professor)	In economics class today, I'll be talking about zero-sum games. Theoretically, zero-sum games are a part of gaming theory, but the concept of zero-sum games has applications in a variety of academic areas. We'll be talking today first about the theoretical concept of zero-sum games and later about its application, of course, in the field of economics.
	Theoretically, a zero-sum game is a game where the total number of points is fixed. If two players, players A and B, are playing a zero-sum game with a total of 100 points possible, then A and B each play to win the highest number of the 100 points available. If A wins 60 points, then B wins the remaining 40 points; if A wins 25 points, then B wins the remaining 75 points.
	A non-zero-sum game is the opposite, a game where the total number of points is not fixed. In one game, perhaps player A wins 20 points and player B wins 30 points for a total of 50 points; in another game A wins 80 points and B wins 70 points for a total of 150 points.
	Now let's take this gaming theory, the zero-sum gaming theory, and apply it to economics. Let's think first about a

zero-sum economic system. In a zero-sum economy, there's a <u>fixed</u> amount of resources. In this economy, A has some of the resources and B has the rest. If A wants more in a zero-sum economy, the only way to get more is to take from B because there's only a fixed amount and B has whatever A doesn't have.

In a non-zero-sum economic system, the total amount of resources is <u>not fixed</u>; more resources can be created. If A has a certain amount of resources, A can either take some resources from B or can simply create more resources because the total amount of resources isn't fixed.

Your assignment for tomorrow is to look at the different economic theories we've been discussing so far—they're listed on page 20 in the text if you don't remember what they are. Look at the different theories in terms of the gaming theory I've just talked about and decide whether you think each of these theories is based upon the belief that the economy is a zero-sum economy or a non-zero-sum economy.

HOW IS THE CONCEPT OF ZERO-SUM GAMES RELATED TO THE STUDY OF ECONOMIC SYSTEMS?

SPEAKING MINI-TEST 6

Page 76
Question 2

Listen to the passage. On a piece of paper, take notes on the main points of the listening passage.

(professor) It's not clear to scientists exactly how this layered structure came to be. The various theories about how the layered structure came about can be classified into two general categories. In one category of theories about how the layered structure came to be, the core formed first and then the lighter layers came later. In the second category of theories, all the material clumped together first and then later separated into layers. In other words, in the first category of theories the Earth started out only as the core, with the lighter layers coming later, and in the second category of theories the Earth started out with all of its material and later separated into layers.

HOW DOES THE INFORMATION IN THE LISTENING PASSAGE ADD TO WHAT IS EXPLAINED IN THE READING PASSAGE?

Page 77
Question 3

Listen to the passage. On a piece of paper, take notes on the main points of the listening passage.

(woman) Hey, Lee, are you going to the outdoor theater tonight?

(man) What for? Is something going on there tonight?

(woman) A guest speaker you said you wanted to go listen to is going to be there.

(man) Which one? I didn't know about any guest speaker at the outdoor theater tonight.

(woman) You know, the guest speaker from the governor's office. You said you wanted to go hear him speak.

(man) But I thought that wasn't until next week. He's scheduled to speak next week. Not tonight.

(woman) No, really. He's going to be speaking at the outdoor theater tonight. I just saw a notice posted over by the theater, and it said he would be speaking tonight.

(man) Wow, I really thought it was next week. I have it written on my calendar that it's next week.

(woman) I actually thought it was scheduled for next week, too.

(man) You know, I really think the schedule must've been changed if we both thought it was next week and not tonight.

(woman) Yeah, the schedule must've been changed, but if it was, then no one did a very good job of letting people know. There's just a sign over at the theater, but most people won't see it until it's too late.

(man) I think we really should let our friends know.

(woman) That sounds like a good idea. Maybe they don't know the speaker's tonight, either.

HOW ARE THE STUDENTS DEALING WITH THE SITUATION SURROUNDING THE GUEST SPEAKER?

SPEAKING MINI-TEST 7

Page 79
Question 2

Listen to the passage. On a piece of paper, take notes on the main points of the listening passage.

(woman) Brian, did you see the part of the syllabus about discussion in class?

(man) I sure did!

(woman) Do you think the professor means it? I mean, it sounds so strict.

(man) I'm actually really sure she means it.

(woman) Really? Why are you so sure?

(man) Because I know someone who took a class from this professor last year. One of my friends did.

(woman) And what did your friend tell you about the class?

(man) He said the professor really makes the point that she wants everyone to read the material and come prepared to take part in the discussion. Each day, the professor starts the class by asking students questions about the reading. If any students can't answer the questions, she tells them to leave the classroom before the discussion starts.

(woman) I guess she is serious about this. I think I'll go to the library and work on the first reading assignment.

(man) From what I've heard, that would be a very sensible idea.

HOW DO THE STUDENTS SEEM TO FEEL ABOUT THE PROFESSOR'S POLICY ON CLASS DISCUSSIONS?

Page 80
Question 3

Listen to the passage. On a piece of paper, take notes on the main points of the listening passage.

(professor) When governments want to construct facilities of some kind, particularly those with some sort of negative effect on their surroundings, they commonly encounter a problem that's now called, simply, NIMBY. That's N-I-M-B-Y, NIMBY. Can you guess what the letters N-I-M-B-Y stand for? Well, they stand for not-in-my-backyard. So, governments encounter the NIMBY response when they want to construct a facility that might have a negative impact on the community where it's built, a facility such as a prison, a landfill, a mental hospital, or a power plant in a community. The community wants these facilities somewhere; communities want facilities like prisons, landfills, mental hospitals, and power plants somewhere, but not in their communities, or NIMBY. When a government announces, for example, that planning for a new prison in a certain area is underway, a strong NIMBY reaction to the news can be expected. This NIMBYism might take the form of neighborhood meetings, demonstrations, picketing, letters to newspapers, letter-writing campaigns directed at decision-making officials, or confrontational meetings with these officials.

WHAT POINTS DOES THE PROFESSOR MAKE ABOUT A CERTAIN KIND OF RESPONSE FROM THE PUBLIC?

SPEAKING MINI-TEST 8

Page 82
Question 2

Listen to the passage. On a piece of paper, take notes on the main points of the listening passage.

(professor) There are several common misconceptions about sonnambulism, or sleepwalking, and I'd like to talk about two of them now.

One common misconception about sleepwalking is that someone who is sleepwalking should not be awakened. Many people will say that it's dangerous to awaken someone who's sleepwalking, but this is not true. It's not really dangerous to awaken someone who's sleepwalking.

Another common misconception about sleepwalking is that someone who's sleepwalking can't get hurt. This is also not true. Someone who's sleepwalking can easily get hurt by running into something or by tripping and falling.

HOW DOES THE INFORMATION IN THE LISTENING PASSAGE ADD TO WHAT IS EXPLAINED IN THE READING PASSAGE?

Page 83
Question 3

Listen to the passage. On a piece of paper, take notes on the main points of the listening passage.

(man) Hey, Tina, you took Dr. Hall's sociology class last year, didn't you?

(woman) Yes, I did.

(man) And you liked it?

(woman) Not at first, but later on I did.

(man) Really? I've just started his class, and I don't like it at all. What made you change your mind about it?

(woman) It wasn't that I changed my mind about it. It's that the class changed, and I liked it better later on. At first, I didn't understand very much of the class at all.

(man) That's the problem I'm having now. How did the class change when you took it?

(woman) Well, it wasn't that the class changed on its own. We students caused the class to change.

(man) How did you do that?

(woman) We started asking questions, asking a lot of questions. Do any of you ask any questions?

(man) We can't. There's not any time to do that. Dr. Hall just charges on and on. He doesn't even seem to stop to take a breath.

(woman) I know what you mean. If no one asks any questions, he just assumes that everyone understands everything. For the first few weeks of my class, no one asked any questions, and he just moved so fast.

(man) And how did you change that?

(woman) Well, after a couple of weeks, someone started asking questions, and Dr. Hall answered them. Pretty soon, we all figured out that we were supposed to ask questions, lots of questions, to keep him from going so fast.

(man) But nobody asks any questions because he's going so fast.

(woman) You just need to start asking questions. At first Dr. Hall will seem a bit surprised because nobody has asked any questions so far, but he'll answer your question, and then ask another question.

(man) And another after that.

(woman) Exactly. That's how you get him to slow down.

WHAT POSSIBLE SOLUTIONS DOES THE WOMAN OFFER TO THE MAN'S PROBLEM?

SPEAKING COMPLETE TEST 1

Page 86
Question 3

Listen to the passage. On a piece of paper, take notes on the main points of the listening passage.

(man) Have you gotten your tickets yet?

(woman) What tickets?

(man) The tickets for the Spring Show. . . . Didn't you see the notice?

(woman) I didn't see any notice, and I don't even know what the Spring Show is.

(man) Oh, you must be new to the school this year.

(woman) I am. I just transferred here this year . . . but how did you know that?

(man) Because anyone who's been here for a while knows what the Spring Show is. It's a really big event.

(woman) I understand that from what you're saying. But do I really need to get tickets now?

(man) Absolutely, if you want to get tickets. Tickets went on sale last Monday, and any remaining tickets will go on sale to the public next Monday. After tickets go on sale to the public, they sell out almost immediately.

(woman) I don't know exactly what the Spring Show is, but it sounds like I should get tickets right away and find out what it is.

(man) Trust me, you won't regret it.

HOW DO THE STUDENTS REACT TO THE NOTICE ABOUT THE SPRING SHOW?

Page 87
Question 4

Listen to the passage. On a piece of paper, take notes on the main points of the listening passage.

(professor) I'm sure you understand from the text that the great apes are able to communicate in a variety of ways within their species. I'd like to talk now about what studies have shown to be some of the limitations of their communication, in particular in two ways that are referred to as a lack of displacement and a lack of productivity.

First, let me talk about a lack of displacement. In terms of communication, a lack of displacement means that the great apes communicate only about things that are physically present. They do not communicate about things that are not physically present. This inability to communicate about things that aren't within range of their senses is called a lack of displacement.

Now, let me talk about a lack of productivity. In terms of communication, a lack of productivity is an inability to manipulate communication, to combine gestures and sounds or use gestures and sounds in different ways to create new meanings. Because the great apes do not manipulate their sounds and gestures to create new meanings, they're said to have a lack of productivity in their communication.

HOW DOES THE INFORMATION IN THE LISTENING PASSAGE ADD TO WHAT IS EXPLAINED IN THE READING PASSAGE?

Page 88
Question 5

Listen to the passage. On a piece of paper, take notes on the main points of the listening passage.

(man) Hey, Tina, what's up? You don't look too happy.

(woman) Oh, I've been trying to choose my classes for next semester.

(man) And that's a problem? You don't like choosing your classes for next semester? I actually enjoy doing that.

(woman) Sometimes I enjoy it, but not this time.

(man) Why not?

(woman) Because I've put off taking some of my required classes, a science class in particular, and now I can't put it off any longer. I have to take a science class next semester.

(man) You're dreading taking a science class? That doesn't sound too terrible to me.

(woman) It doesn't? Have you taken any science classes yet? Maybe you can recommend one to me.

(man) I haven't taken any science classes yet, but I'm looking forward to taking some.

(woman) You are? Really? I don't like science.

(man) But all you have to do is take one science class, and there're so many to choose from, I mean you can take astronomy, or oceanography, or health, or physiology, or geography, or environmental studies. There are so many interesting science classes to choose from.

(woman) (unsure) I guess so. . . .

(man) You know, you really might enjoy one of these science classes. I think you've made such a big deal about taking a science class that you're dreading it, but you might actually enjoy it if you think more positively about it.

(woman) OK, I'll try to do that.

(man) Listen, why don't you let me know what science class you decide to take, and then maybe I'll sign up for the same course, and we can take it together.

(woman) Now, that sounds like a good idea. I'll do that.

HOW IS THE WOMAN DEALING WITH THE PROBLEM SHE IS FACING?

Page 88
Question 6

Listen to the passage. On a piece of paper, take notes on the main points of the listening passage.

(professor) Today, I'll be discussing the economic policy known as mercantilism. Mercantilism was the overriding economic policy of major trading nations for almost two centuries, from the last part of the sixteenth century through the beginning of the eighteenth century, or from the 1580s through the 1720s. Mercantilism. Do you understand this word? It sounds kind of like the word "merchant," and it's related in meaning to the word "merchant." Mercantilism was an economic policy of nations based on developing international business, a policy dedicated to encouraging business production and to encouraging trade between nations.

The goal of mercantilism wasn't simply for nations to encourage business or for nations to try to trade with other nations; and the goal of a mercantilist society wasn't merely to achieve a balance of trade, for each nation to try to balance its imports and exports. Instead, each mercantilist nation was dedicated to amassing national wealth, and to do this each nation wanted to export more than it imported. Any goods that were exported over and above the amount of goods that were imported would be paid for in gold. It was this amassing of gold in payment for exports in excess of imports that would allow a nation to build wealth.

HOW DOES THE PROFESSOR DESCRIBE MERCANTILISM?

SPEAKING COMPLETE TEST 2

Page 91
Question 3

Listen to the passage. On a piece of paper, take notes on the main points of the listening passage.

(man) Have you seen the notice about the internships?
(woman) I have. So?
(man) Are you going to apply for the internship program?
(woman) I don't think so.
(man) Why not? It sounds like a great program to me.

(woman) It does? But it's a lot of work, and there's no pay. If I get a job, I want it to be a job that pays something.
(man) But this isn't for pay. It's for units, for graduate units, and for the work experience.
(woman) Oh, we get units for an internship?
(man) Yeah. Three graduate units. I'd much rather work in a company for units and get some actual work experience than study a textbook and take exams on the text.
(woman) The work experience does sound good, I guess. I mean, it would be good to have some work experience already when I begin applying for jobs after I get my degree.
(man) See, it seems like I might have convinced you to apply for an internship.
(woman) I think you have. Getting three graduate units and some work experience sounds good.

HOW DO THE STUDENTS SEEM TO FEEL ABOUT THE INTERNSHIPS OFFERED BY THE BUSINESS DEPARTMENT?

Page 92
Question 4

Listen to the passage. On a piece of paper, take notes on the main points of the listening passage.

(professor) As you should understand from the reading, supersonic jets are jets that fly faster than the speed of sound. Think about this for a moment, that a supersonic jet moves faster than sound moves. What this means is that a person on the ground won't hear a supersonic jet as it approaches because the supersonic jet's moving faster than the speed of sound; the jet will move toward a person faster than any sound it makes moves. When the sound does catch up, it is heard as a sonic boom, a loud booming noise that results from the shock wave produced when a supersonic jet flies by. So, if you hear a sonic boom, it means that a supersonic aircraft has just passed by.

HOW DOES THE INFORMATION IN THE LISTENING PASSAGE ADD TO WHAT IS EXPLAINED IN THE READING PASSAGE?

Page 93
Question 5

Listen to the passage. On a piece of paper, take notes on the main points of the listening passage.

(man) When do you want to start working on our project?
(woman) Right away. We should start on it really soon.
(man) Do we really need to start on it right away?
(woman) It's really a good idea to do that. I know all about this project.
(man) You do? How do you know about it?

(woman) My roommate took the same class last quarter, and I heard all about it then.

(man) What did you hear about it?

(woman) I heard that the professor talks a little bit about the project each week.

(man) That seems about right. He didn't tell us very much about it this week. I mean, he didn't explain all the steps. He just talked about the beginning steps.

(woman) That's right. He'll talk about a few steps each week, if he does it the same way he did last quarter when my roommate took the class.

(man) And you think that we should do the steps he talks about each week?

(woman) Yes, I do. My roommate said that if we do a few steps each week, then the project really isn't a big deal, but if we put everything off and try to do it all at the end it'll be very difficult.

(man) So you think we should do the first steps that the professor has already talked about?

(woman) Yes, we should. We're supposed to find partners first.

(man) And we've done that. We're going to work together, aren't we?

(woman) Of course.

(man) And then we're supposed to decide on a topic.

(woman) And find ten sources on that topic.

(man) And that's what we need to do this week?

(woman) Yes, so let's meet at the library tomorrow and start on that.

(man) Sounds good to me. . . . By the way, is this how your roommate did the project? She did everything step-by-step with her partner?

(woman) No, not exactly. She and her partner put everything off to the end and then really suffered getting the project done. She told me we definitely should <u>not</u> do the project the same way she did.

HOW ARE THE STUDENTS DEALING WITH THE PROJECT THEY ARE WORKING ON?

Page 93

Question 6

Listen to the passage. On a piece of paper, take notes on the main points of the listening passage.

(professor) Today, I'll be talking about the psychological disorder known as multiple personality disorder. As you can most likely tell from the name of the disorder, multiple personality disorder is a psychological condition in which one person has two or more distinct and well-developed personalities. These two or more personalities exist simultaneously within a single individual.

It's quite common for the distinct personalities in an individual who suffers from multiple personality disorder to have different names, genders, and ages. It's quite possible that one personality in an individual could be a young female named Mary and another personality could be an older male named Michael.

It's also quite common for the attitudes and behaviors of the different personalities in an individual suffering from multiple personality disorder to be radically different. One personality may be a shy and quiet person who doesn't have any friends and who likes to stay home alone watching television, while the other's an outgoing person who likes to spend time getting to know people at wild parties.

Finally, in cases of multiple personality disorder, it's also quite possible that the different personalities may have different talents, abilities, or knowledge. There have been documented cases of multiple personality disorder where one of the personalities has musical talent that other personalities don't, that one personality knows how to play a card game that other personalities don't, and that one personality knows how to speak a foreign language that other personalities don't.

HOW DOES THE PROFESSOR DESCRIBE MULTIPLE PERSONALITY DISORDER?

ANSWER KEY

SPEAKING DIAGNOSTIC PRE-TEST Page 1

Sample Notes

Question 3 Page 3

TOPIC OF READING PASSAGE: notice about registering for classes in Humanities Department

main points of notice:
- too many students registering for classes without fulfilling prerequisites
- now students need signatures from advisors to register for humanities classes (except intro classes)
- advisors must check that students have fulfilled prerequisites

TOPIC OF LISTENING PASSAGE: student conversation about notice

main points of conversation:
- woman has read the notice but man hasn't
- they each need to go see their advisors
- man wants to read notice first

Question 4 Page 4

TOPIC OF READING PASSAGE: nonverbal communication

definition and examples of nonverbal communication:
- definition (any communication without words)
- examples (smiling, frowning, nodding, shaking head, shaking hands, waving hand)

TOPIC OF LISTENING PASSAGE: two points of clarification about nonverbal communication

points of clarification:
- there can be nonverbal communication without intent
- there cannot be nonverbal communication without communication

Question 5 Page 5

TOPIC OF LISTENING PASSAGE: problem the woman is having with her college French class

what the woman's problem is:
- took 3 years of French in high school
- intermediate French is too difficult (she can't understand anything)

what the man suggests:
- find out if other students have the same problem
- talk with her professor

Question 6 Page 5

LISTENING TOPICS: echolocation used by whales

points about echolocation used by whales:
- only toothed, not toothless, whales use echolocation
- whales send out clicks, clicks reflected from objects back to whales
- whales can learn size, shape, distance, speed, direction

SPEAKING SKILLS

SPEAKING EXERCISE 5 Page 22

Sample Notes

1. TOPIC OF READING PASSAGE: notice on problem with bicycle parking on campus

   main points about the topic:
   - too many students parking bicycles in unauthorized places
   - new policy ticketing bicycles parked in unauthorized places
   - authorized parking for bicycles along east and west sides of campus

2. TOPIC OF READING PASSAGE: message on retirement of professor

   main points about the topic:
   - retiring professor has served at university for 50 years
   - will retire at end of next spring semester
   - praised for commitment to students and for publications

3. TOPIC OF READING PASSAGE: part of a class syllabus on professor's policy against late assignments

   main points about the topic:
   - assignments and due dates listed
   - no late assignment accepted, ever
   - grade on late assignment always zero

SPEAKING EXERCISE 6 Page 25

Sample Notes

1. TOPIC OF LISTENING PASSAGE: student conversation on unhappiness with notice on bicycle parking

   main points about the topic:
   - man has seen notice but woman hasn't
   - neither one is happy about notice
   - it seems unfair to both that they cannot park bicycles near classrooms

2. TOPIC OF LISTENING PASSAGE: student conversation about professor who is retiring

   main points about the topic:
   - both students sorry professor is retiring
   - woman's father took classes from professor 30 years ago
   - both students want to take class from professor spring semester

3. TOPIC OF LISTENING PASSAGE: student conversation about part of class syllabus on late assignments

main points about the topic:
- man initially does not believe what syllabus says about late assignments
- woman tells story about injured student whose late papers were not accepted
- man then believes what syllabus says about late papers

SPEAKING EXERCISE 7 Page 28
Sample Notes

1. reading passage describes a *notice*; listening passage shows *students' unhappiness* about the notice

2. reading passage describes a *message about a professor*; listening passage shows *students' reaction* to the message

3. reading passage describes part of a *syllabus*; listening passage shows *students' reaction* to the part of the syllabus

SPEAKING EXERCISE 8 Page 30
Sample Answers

1. In this set of materials, the reading passage is a notice, and the listening passage shows some students' unhappiness with the notice.

   The reading passage is a notice on a problem with bicycle parking on campus. The notice states that too many students are parking bicycles in unauthorized places, that there is a new policy ticketing bicycles parked in unauthorized places, and that the only authorized parking for their bicycles is along two sides of campus.

   The listening passage is a conversation between students who are unhappy with the notice on bicycle parking. In the conversation, the woman has already seen the notice, but the man hasn't. Neither one is happy about the notice because it seems unfair to both of them that they can't park their bicycles near their classrooms.

2. In this set of materials, the reading passage is a message about a professor, and the listening passage shows some students' reaction to the message.

   The reading topic is a message on the retirement of a long-time professor. The message states that the professor who is retiring has served at the university for almost 50 years and will retire at the end of next spring semester. Throughout her career, the professor has been praised for her commitment to students and for her publications.

   The listening topic is a student conversation about the professor who is retiring. In the conversation, both students are sorry the professor is retiring. The woman's father took classes from the same professor 30 years ago, and both students want to take a class from the professor in the coming spring semester.

3. In this set of materials, the reading passage describes part of a syllabus, and the listening passage shows the students' reaction to that part of the syllabus.

The reading passage is part of a class syllabus on a professor's policy against late assignments. The reading passage lists assignments and due dates. It also states that no late assignments are accepted, ever, and that the grade on any late assignment is always zero.

The listening passage is a student conversation about the part of the class syllabus on late assignments. In the conversation, the man initially does not believe what the syllabus says about late assignments. Then the woman tells a story about an injured student whose late papers were not accepted, and the man then believes what the syllabus says about late papers.

SPEAKING REVIEW EXERCISE (Skills 5–8) Page 30
Sample Notes

TOPIC OF READING PASSAGE: part of history syllabus on research assignment

main points about the research assignment:
- students must choose event or person from history
- students must research the event or person
- students must write about the event or person from positive and negative perspectives

TOPIC OF LISTENING PASSAGE: student conversation about research assignment

main points about the conversation:
- man has better understanding of assignment than woman
- man gives reasons why he thinks the professor gave this assignment (students should look at various sources, students should understand that a person or event can be viewed in different ways)

Sample Answer

In this set of materials, the reading passage is part of a syllabus, and the listening passage is a student conversation about this part of the syllabus.

The reading passage is about a research assignment or part of the history syllabus. The main points about the syllabus are that students must choose an event or person from history, they must research the event or person, and they must write about the event or person from positive and negative perspectives.

The listening passage is a student conversation about the research assignment. In the conversation, the man has a better understanding of the assignment than the woman. The man gives reasons why he thinks the professor gave this assignment; the reasons are that the students should look at various sources and that the students should understand that a person or event can be viewed in different ways.

SPEAKING EXERCISE 9 Page 32
Sample Notes

1. TOPIC OF READING PASSAGE: the Dead Sea

   main points about the topic:
   - "dead" because high salt level prevents life in it
   - landlocked with no outlet
   - in area with high temperature, which causes rapid evaporation

2. TOPIC OF READING PASSAGE: polling

   <u>main points about the topic:</u>
   • involves asking people how they feel about an issue or candidate
   • representative sample can be polled if the group to be polled is too large

3. TOPIC OF READING PASSAGE: Polynesian migration in the Pacific Ocean

   <u>details about the topic:</u>
   • started 4,000 years ago
   • covered 20,000 square miles of Pacific Ocean (Hawaii to New Zealand to Easter Island)
   • made use of outrigger canoes (2 tree trunks joined with a platform)

SPEAKING EXERCISE 10 Page 34
Sample Notes

1. TOPIC OF LISTENING PASSAGE: additional point about Dead Sea: Dead Sea is not a sea

   <u>main points about the topic:</u>
   • sea is body of water that is part of ocean or opens into ocean
   • lake is body of water that is entirely enclosed
   • Dead Sea has no outlet and is therefore lake

2. TOPIC OF LISTENING PASSAGE: push polling

   <u>main points about the topic:</u>
   • negative and unfair kind of polling
   • involves asking leading questions to influence person being polled

3. TOPIC OF LISTENING PASSAGE: one special aspect of Polynesian migration: Polynesians may have made it to South America

   <u>main points about the topic:</u>
   • surprising because they were traveling on outrigger canoes
   • South American plants in Hawaii may be indication this happened

SPEAKING EXERCISE 11 Page 37

1. reading passage describes *a body of water*; listening passage provides *additional information* about the body of water

2. reading passage describes *polling in general*; listening passage describes *one specific kind of polling*

3. reading passage describes *a migration by one culture*; listening passage describes *one special aspect of that migration*

SPEAKING EXERCISE 12 Page 39
Sample Answers

1. In this set of materials, the reading passage describes a body of water, and the listening passage provides additional information about the body of water.

   The reading passage describes the body of water named the Dead Sea. This body of water is said to be "dead" because its high salt level prevents life in it. It's so salty because it's landlocked with no outlet and it's in an area with a high temperature, which causes rapid evaporation.

The listening passage makes an additional point about the Dead Sea. This point is that the Dead Sea isn't really a sea. A sea is a body of water that's part of the ocean or opens into the ocean, while a lake is a body of water that's entirely enclosed. The Dead Sea has no outlet and is therefore a lake.

2. In this set of materials, the reading passage describes polling in general, and the listening passage describes one specific kind of polling.

   The reading passage describes polling, which is a process that involves asking people how they feel about an issue or candidate. A representative sample can be polled if the group to be polled is too large.

   The listening passage describes one particular kind of polling, which is called push polling. Push polling is a negative and unfair kind of polling that involves asking leading questions to influence the person being polled.

3. In this set of materials, the reading passage describes a migration by one culture, and the listening passage describes one special aspect of that migration.

   The reading passage describes the Polynesian migration across the Pacific Ocean. This migration started 4,000 years ago and covered 20,000 square miles of Pacific Ocean, from Hawaii to New Zealand to Easter Island. This migration was accomplished using outrigger canoes, which consisted of two tree trunks joined with a platform.

   The listening passage describes one special aspect of Polynesian migration. This special aspect is that the Polynesians may have made it to South America, which would be surprising because the Polynesians were traveling on outrigger canoes. One indication that this might have happened is that there are plants from South America in Hawaii.

SPEAKING REVIEW EXERCISE (Skills 9–12) Page 39
Sample Notes

   TOPIC OF READING PASSAGE: equity theory of employee satisfaction

   <u>main points about equity theory:</u>
   • employee determines return for contribution and compares their return for contribution to other employees
   • employee content if return for contribution is higher than or equal to return for contribution of other employees and unhappy if it is lower

   TOPIC OF LISTENING PASSAGE: examples of equity theory

   <u>examples related to employee X:</u>
   • employee X satisfied when he and coworker have equal returns for contributions (similar job title, work, salary, office)
   • employee X dissatisfied when he gets less return for contribution than coworker (same job title but more work, less money, smaller office)

Sample Answer

   In this set of materials, the reading passage describes a theory, and the listening passage provides examples of this theory.

The reading passage describes the equity theory of employee satisfaction. According to this theory, the employee determines his or her return for contribution and compares it to the return for contribution of other employees. An employee will be content if his or her return for contribution is higher than or equal to the return for contribution of other employees and unhappy if it is lower.

The listening passage provides examples of the equity theory of employee satisfaction. In the first example, employee X is satisfied when he and his coworker have equal returns for their contributions such as similar job titles, similar work, similar salaries, and similar offices. In the second example, employee X is dissatisfied when he receives less return for contribution than his coworker, such as having the same job title but having to do more work, making less money, and having a smaller office.

SPEAKING EXERCISE 13 Page 42
Sample Notes

1. TOPIC OF LISTENING PASSAGE: woman wants to know about two different professors who teach the same course

   main points about what the woman learns about the two professors:
   • Dr. Abbott has interesting discussions and gives essay exams
   • Dr. Becker concentrates on details and gives multiple-choice exams

   main points about what the woman thinks about the two professors:
   • interesting discussions sound good but essay exams do not
   • concentration on details doesn't sound good but multiple-choice exams do

2. TOPIC OF LISTENING PASSAGE: man unable to go to big game because he needs to review notes for an exam

   main points about what woman suggests to the man:
   • review and reorganize notes soon after taking them
   • not wait until just before exam to review notes

   main points about what man decides:
   • can try this method with future notes
   • needs to review old notes now and can't go to game

3. TOPIC OF LISTENING PASSAGE: woman's question about an independent study project

   what the man says he did wrong:
   • put off the project until a couple of days before each monthly meeting
   • expected professor to tell him what to do

   what the woman should do:
   • work on project regularly throughout each month
   • determine direction research should go and discuss ideas with professor

SPEAKING EXERCISE 14 Page 45

1. woman learns about the teaching styles of two professors and states what she thinks about the two styles

2. woman offers suggestion to help man solve a problem, and he reacts to this

3. woman learns how man completed a project and learns from what he says

SPEAKING EXERCISE 15 Page 47
Sample Answers

1. In this listening passage, the woman learns about the teaching styles of two professors and states what she thinks about the two styles.

   The woman wants to know about two different professors who teach the same course. She learns that Dr. Abbott has a lot of interesting discussions and gives essay exams and that Dr. Becker concentrates on details and gives multiple-choice exams.

   After the woman learns about the two professors, she comes to the conclusion that interesting discussions sound good but essay exams do not and that concentration on details doesn't sound good but multiple-choice exams do.

2. In this listening passage, the woman offers a suggestion to the man to help him solve a problem he is having, and the man reacts to her suggestion.

   The situation is that the man is unable to go to a big game because he needs to review his notes before an exam. The woman suggests that the man review and reorganize his notes soon after taking them and that he not wait until just before an exam to review his notes.

   After this discussion, the man decides that he can try this method with his notes in the future but that he needs to review his old notes now and he cannot go to the game.

3. In this listening passage, the woman learns how the man completed a project, and she learns what she should do from what he says.

   The woman asks the man about an independent study project he worked on with Dr. Lee. The man tells the woman that the two problems he had were that he put off working on the project until a couple of days before each monthly meeting and that he expected the professor to tell him what to do.

   After she hears this, the woman comes to the conclusion that she should work on the project regularly throughout each month and that she should determine the direction her research should go and then discuss her ideas with the professor.

SPEAKING REVIEW EXERCISE (Skills 13–15) Page 47
Sample Notes

TOPIC OF LISTENING PASSAGE: man's boredom in class because of lack of involvement

how man shows he's bored:
• sits in the back
• almost falls asleep

how woman suggests that he can become more involved:
• should sit in the front
• should answer questions and ask the professor questions

Sample Answer

In this listening passage, the man describes a problem he's having in a certain class, and the woman offers suggestions to solve the problem.

The problem the man has is that he's bored in class. The man shows that he's bored by sitting in the back of the classroom and almost falling asleep.

The woman suggests that the man can take specific steps to become more involved in the class. He can try sitting in the front of the classroom. He can also answer questions the professor asks and ask the professor questions.

SPEAKING EXERCISE 16 Page 49
Sample Notes

1. TOPIC OF LISTENING PASSAGE: Bank Holiday of 1933

   main points about the Bank Holiday of 1933:
   • was not a holiday (was a closing of unstable banks)
   • banks were closed while federal government reorganized the banking system
   • one part of reorganization was federal deposit insurance
   • since then bank failures have decreased considerably

2. TOPIC OF LISTENING PASSAGE: definition of creativity

   main points in definition of creativity:
   • originality (idea must not be normal, everyday idea)
   • appropriateness (idea must fit the situation)

3. TOPIC OF LISTENING PASSAGE: how the Amazon River got its name

   two sources contributed to its name:
   • native inhabitants gave river the name Amanuzu ("big wave")
   • chronicle by European explorers describes female warriors who resembled Amazons in Greek literature

SPEAKING EXERCISE 17 Page 52

1. professor describes Bank Holiday of 1933

2. professor discusses definition of creativity

3. professor discusses how the Amazon river got its name

SPEAKING EXERCISE 18 Page 54
Sample Answers

1. In this listening passage, a professor describes the Bank Holiday of 1933. The main point the professor makes about the Bank Holiday of 1933 is that it was not a holiday but was instead a closing of unstable banks. Banks were closed while the federal government reorganized the banking system. One part of the reorganization was federal deposit insurance, and since then, bank failures have decreased considerably.

2. In this listening passage, a professor discusses a definition of creativity. The point the professor makes about this definition is that it must include the ideas of originality and appropriateness. Originality means

that a creative idea must not be a normal, everyday idea, and appropriateness means that a creative idea must fit the situation.

3. In this listening passage, a professor discusses how the Amazon River got its name. Two sources contributed to its name. The first source is the name given to the river by native inhabitants; this name was Amanuzu, which meant "big wave." The second source was a chronicle by European explorers. This chronicle described female warriors who resembled Amazons in Greek literature.

SPEAKING REVIEW EXERCISE (Skills 16–18) Page 54
Sample Notes

TOPIC OF LISTENING PASSAGE: seasonal affective disorder (SAD)

main points about SAD:
• affects people living in areas where sunlight is low in winter (such as Alaska)
• reduced sunlight causes reduced serotonin (hormone that causes cheerfulness) and increased melatonin (hormone that causes sleepiness)

Sample Answer

In this listening passage, the professor discusses seasonal affective disorder, or SAD. The professor makes the point that SAD affects people living in areas where sunlight is low in winter, such as Alaska. The reduced sunlight causes reduced serotonin, which is a hormone that causes cheerfulness, and increased melatonin, which is a hormone that causes sleepiness.

SPEAKING POST-TEST Page 55
Sample Notes

Question 3 Page 57

TOPIC OF READING PASSAGE: problem at the university's main cafeteria

main points about the topic:
• main cafeteria closed from October 24 to November 1
• students with meal cards can use them at 3 snack bars on campus

TOPIC OF LISTENING PASSAGE: student discussion of the problem at the cafeteria

main points about the topic:
• both man and woman are going to snack bar for lunch
• man saw the notice and woman heard about it
• man can't believe cafeteria is closed during the semester
• woman heard cafeteria is closed because of a fire

Question 4 Page 58

TOPIC OF READING PASSAGE: importance for a teacher to choose appropriate social environment in the classroom

types of social environments:
• cooperative = students work together to come up with best answers together

- competitive = students work alone to come up with better answers than other students
- individualistic = students work alone to come up with best answers individually

TOPIC OF LISTENING PASSAGE: how a teacher can establish different social environments

ways to establish social environments:
- cooperative (by putting students in pairs or groups and accepting only answers that have been agreed upon by group)
- competitive (by having students work individually and evaluating responses in comparison with answers from other students)
- individualistic (by having students work individually and evaluating responses based upon a predetermined scale)

Question 5 Page 59

TOPIC OF LISTENING PASSAGE: student conversation about woman's class schedule

main points about the topic:
- woman scheduled four classes in a row in different corners of university and cannot get to her classes on time
- man suggests thinking about where classes meet, not just when

Question 6 Page 59

TOPIC OF LISTENING PASSAGE: one reason people thought there were living beings on Mars

a linguistic error:
- Italian astronomer saw *canali* on Mars in 1877
- *canali* in Italian can be natural or man-made
- in English canals are man-made and channels are natural
- *canali* was translated into English as "canals" (man-made)
- conclusion was that astronomer said there were living beings on Mars

SPEAKING MINI-TEST 1   Page 60

Sample Notes

Question 2 Page 61

TOPIC OF READING PASSAGE: part of syllabus on assignment to watch films

main points about assignment:
- given list of 20 films
- must watch at least 12 films
- students write a report summarizing each film they watch
- may turn in extra reports for extra credit

TOPIC OF LISTENING PASSAGE: student conversation about assignment to watch films

how students seem to feel about assignment:
- man initially thinks assignment is too much work
- woman is enthusiastic about assignment
- man finally decides assignment not so bad (summaries not too bad, there are worse assignments than watching films)

Question 3 Page 62

TOPIC OF LISTENING PASSAGE: formation of glaciers (masses of moving ice)

how glaciers form:
- considerable snow accumulates
- pressure on snow underneath causes change to small ice crystals
- pressure causes small ice crystals to become large ice crystals
- large amount of crystallized ice begins to move

SPEAKING MINI-TEST 2   Page 63

Sample Notes

Question 2 Page 64

TOPIC OF READING PASSAGE: group leadership

two types of group leadership:
- instrumental leadership (concern with getting tasks done)
- expressive leadership (concern for the well-being of group)

TOPIC OF LISTENING PASSAGE: examples of group leadership

two situations showing different types of group leadership:
- group 1 had expressive leadership (activities to get to know each other, positive comments about project, e-mail describing feelings)
- group 2 had instrumental leadership (detailed list of work to be done, meetings about what was and was not accomplished, emphasis on getting work done on time)

Question 3 Page 65

TOPIC OF LISTENING PASSAGE: student conversation about attending an open student council meeting

main points of discussion:
- meeting will be about changing final exam schedule
- proposed change from six to three days
- students who support change want earlier summer vacation
- both oppose change because both have five exams
- both decide to attend meeting to voice opinions

SPEAKING MINI-TEST 3   Page 66

Sample Notes

Question 2 Page 67

TOPIC OF READING PASSAGE: notice about rules in the library

library rules:
- reading, working on research, or studying only
- no music, no talking, no sleeping, no eating or drinking

TOPIC OF LISTENING PASSAGE: student conversation about notice

how students feel about notice:
• woman is happy about new rules (she wants to study in peace and quiet)
• man is unhappy about notice (he wants to talk, sleep, eat and drink, play music while studying)

Question 3 Page 68

TOPIC OF LISTENING PASSAGE: attempt during neoclassic period to make English more like Latin

main points of this attempt:
• during neoclassic period (17th and 18th centuries) high regard for ancient Greeks and Romans
• academics tried to make English more like Latin
• an example = rule in English against split infinitives

SPEAKING MINI-TEST 4 Page 69

Sample Notes

Question 2 Page 70

TOPIC OF READING PASSAGE: issue of nullification

what nullification is:
• doctrine by which states believed they could refuse to accept federal laws
• federal government did not believe states could nullify federal laws

TOPIC OF LISTENING PASSAGE: situation when issue of nullification arose

main points about the situation:
• in 1828 federal government authorized tariffs on some imported goods
• one southern state refused to pay tariffs (nullified federal law)
• federal government sent troops to southern state
• compromise lowering tariffs was reached to resolve situation

Question 3 Page 71

TOPIC OF LISTENING PASSAGE: student conversation about a paper for psychology class

main points about the paper:
• man wrote simple, direct answer to question
• man's paper was praised by professor
• woman wrote creative answer to question
• woman's paper was not praised by professor (professor wrote "needs work")
• woman decides to write simple, direct answer instead of creative answer in next paper

SPEAKING MINI-TEST 5 Page 72

Sample Notes

Question 2 Page 73

TOPIC OF READING PASSAGE: announcement of positions for student assistants in Administration Building

requirement for positions:
• full-time with at least 60 units
• 3.0 minimum grade-point average
• mornings or afternoons Monday–Friday
• computer and telephone skills
• application submitted by Friday afternoon

TOPIC OF LISTENING PASSAGE: woman discusses applying for position with man

woman doesn't meet most requirements:
• has only 45 not 60 units
• has a 2.5 grade-point average not 3.0
• not available every morning or afternoon
• has telephone skills but not computer skills
• already submitted application anyway
• man thinks it is a waste of her time

Question 3 Page 74

TOPIC OF LISTENING PASSAGE: zero-sum game theory and application in economics

theory:
• total points fixed in zero-sum game
• total points not fixed in non-zero-sum game

application of theory to economics:
• total resources fixed in zero-sum economy
• total resources not fixed in non-zero-sum economy

SPEAKING MINI-TEST 6 Page 75

Sample Notes

Question 2 Page 76

TOPIC OF READING PASSAGE: how our solar system and our planet were formed

main points of formation of solar system and Earth:
• solar system started as spinning cloud of dust and gas
• dust and gas began clumping together
• majority of dust and gas became Sun
• smaller clumps became planets
• Earth formed globe with layered structure
• heavier material in middle and lighter material on the outside

TOPIC OF LISTENING PASSAGE: how the layered structure of our planet was formed

two categories of theories:
• the core formed first and the lighter layers came later
• material clumped first and layers formed later

Question 3 Page 77

TOPIC OF LISTENING PASSAGE: student conversation about a guest speaker tonight

main points about the conversation:
• woman saw sign saying guest speaker will appear tonight
• both thought speaker was next week
• both think schedule must have been changed
• both decide to let friends know about change

SPEAKING MINI-TEST 7 Page 78

Sample Notes

Question 2 Page 79

TOPIC OF READING PASSAGE: part of syllabus describing professor's policy on preparation for class discussions

professor's policy:
- students must complete assigned reading before class
- must take part in class discussions
- should not come to class if they have not completed the reading
- should not come to class if they are not going to take part in class discussion

TOPIC OF LISTENING PASSAGE: students' reaction to policy on preparation for class discussions

students' reaction:
- woman at first questions policy
- man explains that he knows policy is real from friend who took class
- woman comes to believe that policy is real

Question 3 Page 80

TOPIC OF LISTENING PASSAGE: problem called NIMBY (not-in-my-backyard)

situation with NIMBY:
- response when government wants to construct facility that will impact community (prison, landfill, mental hospital, power plant)
- citizens want these facilities but somewhere else
- NIMBY takes form of meetings, demonstrations, picketing, letter writing

SPEAKING MINI-TEST 8 Page 81

Sample Notes

Question 2 Page 82

TOPIC OF READING PASSAGE: characteristics of somnambulism (sleepwalking)

characteristics:
- perhaps caused by fatigue, exhaustion, anxiety, drugs
- may result in simple actions (sitting up, getting up, walking around)
- may result in complex actions (dressing, washing dishes, moving furniture, operating machines)
- may be brief or last more than an hour

TOPIC OF LISTENING PASSAGE: common misconceptions about somnambulism (sleepwalking)

two common misconceptions:
- that it is dangerous to awaken a sleepwalker
- that a sleepwalker can't get hurt

Question 3 Page 83

TOPIC OF LISTENING PASSAGE: student conversation about a problem the man is having in a class

main points about the conversation:
- man taking a class that woman already took
- woman didn't enjoy class at first but did later
- man just starting class and doesn't like it
- problem is that professor goes so fast
- woman says solution is to ask a lot of questions
- professor slows down to answer questions
- man decides to start asking a lot of questions

SPEAKING COMPLETE TEST 1 Page 84

Sample Notes

Question 3 Page 86

TOPIC OF READING PASSAGE: notice about getting tickets for special show

main points about notice:
- Spring Show is annual event
- tickets go on sale for students on March 1
- remaining tickets go on sale to public on March 8
- tickets always sell out early

TOPIC OF LISTENING PASSAGE: student conversation about getting tickets for Spring Show

what each student thinks:
- woman has not seen notice and does not know about show (because she is new to school)
- man emphasizes that she should see show and should get tickets soon (before they sell out)

Question 4 Page 87

TOPIC OF READING PASSAGE: communication by great apes (gorillas, chimpanzees, orangutans)

characteristics of ape communication:
- communicate in variety of ways (facial expressions, gestures, calls)
- express wide range of ideas (anger, fear, danger, dominance, acceptance)

TOPIC OF LISTENING PASSAGE: limitations of ape communication

two kinds of limitations:
- lack of displacement (communicate only about things that are present)
- lack of productivity (communicate without manipulating to create new meanings)

Question 5 Page 88

TOPIC OF LISTENING PASSAGE: student conversation about woman's schedule for next semester

main points about conversation:
- woman must take a science class next semester
- woman is dreading this class
- man says it is not a problem
- man says there are many science classes to choose from
- man says she should have a more positive attitude about the science class
- man says she should choose a science class and maybe they can take it together
- woman is pleased with man's suggestion

Question 6 Page 88

TOPIC OF LISTENING PASSAGE: mercantilism (economic policy of trading nations from 1580s to 1720s)

main points about mercantilism:
• was based on developing trade between nations
• had as goal to amass national wealth
• created national wealth by receiving payments in gold for exports over imports

SPEAKING COMPLETE TEST 2 Page 89

Sample Notes

Question 3 Page 91

TOPIC OF READING PASSAGE: notice from Business Department on internships

main points about notice:
• some internships in local businesses available
• internships require 10 hours per week for 12 weeks
• students with internships sign up for Business 500
• students submit application and three references

TOPIC OF LISTENING PASSAGE: student conversation about notice on internships

what students think about internships:
• woman not interested in internships at first because there is no pay
• man explains that they get units and experience
• woman changes mind about internships

Question 4 Page 92

TOPIC OF READING PASSAGE: speed of aircraft

main points about speed of aircraft:
• subsonic = slower than speed of sound
• supersonic = faster than speed of sound
• Mach 1 = at speed of sound
• Mach 2 = twice speed of sound

TOPIC OF LISTENING PASSAGE: sound in relation to supersonic aircraft

when sound from supersonic aircraft is heard:
• person on ground will not hear supersonic aircraft before it approaches (it is flying faster than the speed of sound)
• person on ground will hear sonic boom after supersonic aircraft passes (creates a shock wave as it passes)

Question 5 Page 93

TOPIC OF LISTENING PASSAGE: conversation about a project two students are starting

main points about the conversation:
• man and woman working on project together
• woman's roommate did same project last quarter so woman knows about it
• professor gives a few instructions each week
• roommate says it is best to work on a few steps each week
• roommate did not do the project step by step
• man and woman decide to start now on first steps

Question 6 Page 93

TOPIC OF LISTENING PASSAGE: multiple personality disorder (one person with two or more personalities)

characteristics of multiple personalities in one person:
• have different names, genders, and ages (young female Mary versus older male Michael)
• have different personalities (shy and quiet versus outgoing)
• have different talents, abilities, knowledge (musical talent, knowledge of card game, ability to speak foreign language)

AUDIO CD TRACKING LIST

Track	Page	Activity
		CD 1
1		CD 1 Program Introduction
2		CD 1 Title
3	1	Speaking Diagnostic Pre-Test Directions
4	2	Question 1 Preparation
5	2	Question 1 Response
6	2	Question 2 Preparation
7	2	Question 2 Response
8	3	Question 3 Reading Passage
9	3	Question 3 Listening Passage
10	3	Question 3 Preparation
11	3	Question 3 Response
12	4	Question 4 Reading Passage
13	4	Question 4 Listening Passage
14	4	Question 4 Preparation
15	4	Question 4 Response
16	5	Question 5 Listening Passage
17	5	Question 5 Preparation
18	5	Question 5 Response
19	5	Question 6 Listening Passage
20	5	Question 6 Preparation
21	5	Question 6 Response
22	25	Speaking Exercise 6, Question 1
23	25	Speaking Exercise 6, Question 2
24	26	Speaking Exercise 6, Question 3
25	30	Speaking Review Exercise (Skills 5–8) Reading Passage
26	30	Speaking Review Exercise (Skills 5–8) Listening Passage
27	30	Speaking Review Exercise (Skills 5–8) Preparation
28	30	Speaking Review Exercise (Skills 5–8) Response
29	34	Speaking Exercise 10, Question 1
30	35	Speaking Exercise 10, Question 2
31	35	Speaking Exercise 10, Question 3
32	39	Speaking Review Exercise (Skills 9–12) Reading Directions
33	39	Speaking Review Exercise (Skills 9–12) Listening Passage
34	39	Speaking Review Exercise (Skills 9–12) Preparation
35	39	Speaking Review Exercise (Skills 9–12) Response
36	42	Speaking Exercise 13, Question 1
37	42	Speaking Exercise 13, Question 2
38	43	Speaking Exercise 13, Question 3
39	47	Speaking Review Exercise (Skills 13–15) Listening Passage
40	47	Speaking Review Exercise (Skills 13–15) Preparation
41	47	Speaking Review Exercise (Skills 13–15) Response
42	49	Speaking Exercise 16, Question 1
43	50	Speaking Exercise 16, Question 2
44	50	Speaking Exercise 16, Question 3

Track	Page	Activity
45	54	Speaking Review Exercise (Skills 16–18) Listening Passage
46	54	Speaking Review Exercise (Skills 16–18) Preparation
47	54	Speaking Review Exercise (Skills 16–18) Response
		CD 2
1		CD 2 Program Introduction
2	55	Speaking Post-Test Directions
3	56	Question 1 Preparation
4	56	Question 1 Response
5	56	Question 2 Preparation
6	56	Question 2 Response
7	57	Question 3 Reading Directions
8	57	Question 3 Listening Passage
9	57	Question 3 Preparation
10	57	Question 3 Response
11	58	Question 4 Reading Passage
12	58	Question 4 Listening Passage
13	58	Question 4 Preparation
14	58	Question 4 Response
15	59	Question 5 Listening Passage
16	59	Question 5 Preparation
17	59	Question 5 Response
18	59	Question 6 Listening Passage
19	59	Question 6 Preparation
20	59	Question 6 Response
21	60	Speaking Mini-Test 1 Directions
22	61	Question 1 Preparation
23	61	Question 1 Response
24	61	Question 2 Reading Directions
25	61	Question 2 Listening Passage
26	61	Question 2 Preparation
27	61	Question 2 Response
28	62	Question 3 Listening Passage
29	62	Question 3 Preparation
30	62	Question 3 Response
31	63	Speaking Mini-Test 2 Directions
32	64	Question 1 Preparation
33	64	Question 1 Response
34	64	Question 2 Reading Directions
35	64	Question 2 Listening Passage
36	64	Question 2 Preparation
37	64	Question 2 Response
38	65	Question 3 Listening Passage
39	65	Question 3 Preparation
40	65	Question 3 Response
41	66	Speaking Mini-Test 3 Directions
42	67	Question 1 Preparation
43	67	Question 1 Response
44	67	Question 2 Reading Directions
45	67	Question 2 Listening Passage
46	67	Question 2 Preparation
47	67	Question 2 Response
48	68	Question 3 Listening Passage
49	68	Question 3 Preparation

Single User License Agreement:

IMPORTANT: READ CAREFULLY

WARNING: BY OPENING THE PACKAGE YOU AGREE TO BE BOUND BY THE TERMS OF THE LICENSE AGREEMENT BELOW

This is a legally binding agreement between You (the user or purchaser) and Pearson Education, Inc. By retaining this license, any software media or accompanying written materials or carrying out any of the permitted activities You agree to be bound by the terms of the license agreement below. If You do not agree to these terms, then promptly return the entire publication (this license and all software, written materials, packaging and any other components received with it) with Your sales receipt to Your supplier for a full refund.

SINGLE USER LICENSE AGREEMENT

❑ **YOU ARE PERMITTED TO:**

✓ Use (load into temporary memory or permanent storage) a single copy of the software on only one computer at a time. If this computer is linked to a network then the software may only be installed in a manner such that it is not accessible to other machines on the network.

✓ Use the software with a class provided it is only installed on one computer

✓ Transfer the software from one computer to another provided that you only use it on one computer at a time

✓ Print out individual screen extracts from the disk for (a) private study or (b) to include in Your essays or classwork with students

✓ Photocopy individual screen extracts for Your schoolwork or classwork with students

❑ **YOU MAY NOT:**

✗ Rent or lease the software or any part of the publication

✗ Copy any part of the documentation, except where specifically indicated otherwise

✗ Make copies of the software, even for backup purposes

✗ Reverse engineer, decompile or disassemble the software or create a derivative product from the contents of the databases or any software included in them

✗ Use the software on more than one computer at a time

✗ Install the software on any networked computer or server in a way that could allow access to it from more than one machine on the network

✗ Include any material or software from the disk in any other product or software materials except as allowed under "You are permitted to"

✗ Use the software in any way not specified above without prior written consent of the Publisher

✗ Print out more than one page at a time

ONE COPY ONLY

This license is for a single user copy of the software. THE PUBLISHER RESERVES THE RIGHT TO TERMINATE THIS LICENSE BY WRITTEN NOTICE AND TO TAKE ACTION TO RECOVER ANY DAMAGES SUFFERED BY THE PUBLISHER IF YOU BREACH ANY PROVISION OF THIS AGREEMENT.

The Publisher owns the software. You only own the disk on which the software is supplied.

LIMITED WARRANTY

The Publisher warrants that the disk or CD-ROM on which the software is supplied is free from defects in materials and workmanship under normal use for ninety (90) days from the date You received them. This warranty is limited to You and is not transferable. The Publisher does not warrant that the functions of the software meet Your requirements or that the media is compatible with any computer system on which it is used or that the operation of the software will be unlimited or error free.

You assume responsibility for selecting the software to achieve Your intended results and for the installation of, the use of, and the results obtained from the software. The entire liability of the Publisher and Your only remedy shall be replacement free of charge of the components that do not meet this warranty.

This limited warranty is void if any damage has resulted from accident, abuse, misapplication, service or modification by someone other than the Publisher. In no event shall the Publisher or its suppliers be liable for any damages whatsoever arising out of installation of the software, even if advised of the possibility of such damages. The Publisher will not be liable for any loss or damage of any nature suffered by any part as a result of reliance upon or reproduction of any errors in the content of the publication.

The Publisher does not limit its liability for death or personal injury caused by its negligence. This license agreement shall be governed by and interpreted and construed in accordance with New York State law.

For technical assistance, you may call (877) 546-5408 or e-mail epsupport@pearsoned.com.